EDUCATION
FOR
JUSTICE

ORBIS BOOKS
MARYKNOLL   NEW YORK

EDUCATION FOR JUSTICE

A PARTICIPANT WORKBOOK

Edited by THOMAS P. FENTON

*Acknowledgment is gratefully extended
for permission to reprint the following:*

Paul M. Dietterich, *Some Dimensions of International Affairs Education*, Department of International Affairs, National Council of Churches of Christ in the U.S.A.

Julius K. Nyerere, *Division is the Problem of the Third World*.

Thomas P. Fenton, *Coffee: The Rules of the Game and You*, The Christophers.

"Charity/Justice," from *Justice in the World: A Primer for Teachers*, Division for Justice and Peace, United States Catholic Conference.

Richard J. Barnet, *Can the United States Promote Foreign Development?*, Overseas Development Council.

On Trial: An American War, Division for Justice and Peace, United States Catholic Conference.

Every Man My Brother?, Division for Justice and Peace, United States Catholic Conference.

"First Things First," Simulation Sharing Service.

Pope Paul VI, *A Call to Action*, United States Catholic Conference.

Thomas P. Fenton, *The Coffee Game*.

Sonja Anna Hedlund and Betty Strathman Pagett, *The Money Game*.

The Bishops' Call for Peace and the Self-Development of Peoples, General Conference Statement, United Methodist Church.

Synod of Roman Catholic Bishops, *Justice in the World*, United States Catholic Conference.

"Serfdom," People Acting Together for Change of New Detroit, Inc.

L. McCulloch, T. Fenton, E. Toland, *World Justice and Peace: A Radical Analysis for American Christians*.

PHOTO CREDITS:

1: Joseph Vail	62: NASA
5: Kapiassa Nicholas Husseini	64: Colombia National Tourist Board
6: Inocente Salazar	96-97: Donald Bank
9: Agostino Bono	101: Donald Bank
20: John Padula	102: United Nations
28: Donald Casey	104-05: United Nations
32: David D. Duncan, U.S. Marine Corps	112: Gustavo Roa
46: Ralph Looney	

CONTENTS

*"Let justice
roll down like waters,
and righteousness
like an everflowing stream"*

AMOS 5:24

What do I hear?
What am I saying?

**What are the difficulties involved in understanding
beliefs and ways of acting that are not our own?**

Exercise

A. *Place an "x" under either Pro or Con to indicate whether you agree or disagree
with each of the following statements:*

	Pro		Con	
1	_____	Every high school student should be required to take some vocational training during the course of studies.	_____	1
2	_____	We spend too much foreign aid money helping other countries.	_____	2
3	_____	The U.S. should mind its own business in world affairs.	_____	3
4	_____	Our country will become too militarized if we have only an all-volunteer army.	_____	4
5	_____	Men and women should share the housework evenly.	_____	5
6	_____	The use of marijuana should be legalized.	_____	6
7	_____	The inclusion of China in the UN has been a good thing.	_____	7
8	_____	Football as a sport is too violent and competitive.	_____	8
9	_____	There should be a limit to how much wealth any one U.S. citizen can have.	_____	9
10	_____	The race to the moon was a waste of money.	_____	10

B. *Place an "x" on one of the dashes (from 1 to 10) to indicate the degree of your belief in one of the two extreme statements in each of the following.*

> *Note:* A 5 or 6 means that you lean in the direction of the appropriate statement but that you're not very committed to it.

An annual defense budget of even $100 billion would be too small to adequately insure the safety and security of our country.

The more we spend on defense in the U.S. the less secure we feel —so we should do away with all but the very minimum in defense spending.

___ ___ ___ ___ ___   ___ ___ ___ ___ ___
   1   2   3   4   5   6   7   8   9   10

Small handguns should be totally outlawed in the U.S. because they are used so often in violent crimes.

Provided they intend to do no harm to others, persons should be free to buy and use any weapon they want.

___ ___ ___ ___ ___   ___ ___ ___ ___ ___
   1   2   3   4   5   6   7   8   9   10

The United States is fundamentally the most just and democratic society in today's world.

Other countries are as just and democratic as the United States— some are even more so.

___ ___ ___ ___ ___   ___ ___ ___ ___ ___
   1   2   3   4   5   6   7   8   9   10

People are *by nature* aggressive, selfish, and competitive.

People are taught and encouraged by society to be whatever they are—competitive or cooperative, etc.

___ ___ ___ ___ ___   ___ ___ ___ ___ ___
   1   2   3   4   5   6   7   8   9   10

Since the misuse of alcohol leads to so much death and destruction it should be totally prohibited in the U.S.

All restrictions on the sale or use of alcohol in the United States should be removed.

___ ___ ___ ___ ___   ___ ___ ___ ___ ___
   1   2   3   4   5   6   7   8   9   10

3

What do I see?

What do things look like from another point of view?

Exercise

A. *Fill the boxes with words that come to your mind when you hear the word that is beneath each of the boxes.*

WELFARE

COMMUNISM

AFRICAN

JEWISH

How would you expect a person from each of these four categories to react to the words you chose to describe him/her?

4

B.

This is the way one Latin American sees the United States. Is there truth in the way he perceives things? Do you agree or disagree with his perceptions?

C.

What's your first reaction when you see this picture? Would it change your point of view to know that this woman is fighting against Portuguese colonialism in the southern African country of Angola?

5

More than meets the eye

How do we see other cultures and peoples not our own?

Background Reading:

From *Some Dimensions of International Affairs Education* by Paul M. Dietterich.

Instead of finding in the churches a growing, positive love toward self and others, we find prejudice and ethnocentrism, leading to distrust and paranoia.

Gordon Allport, summarizing his research on the psychology of religion and the psychology of prejudice, wrote, "It is a well-established fact in social science that on the average churchgoers in our country harbor more racial, ethnic, and religious prejudice than do non-churchgoers."

The close correlation between prejudice and religious orthodoxy led the author Kirkpatrick to conclude that religion is not a fount of humanitarianism and should not be supported as such. A study of 800 Protestant seminarians reported that the more conservative persons are in their religious ideology, the more they tend to exhibit prejudice against and rejection of such outgroups as Negroes, Jews, and persons of other nations, and to idealize the corresponding ingroups. Conversely, the more liberal the religious ideology, the greater the rejection of outgroup idealization.

One manifestation of prejudice and ethnocentrism verging on paranoia is the present national defensiveness. The proportion of the national budget that goes for military defense appropriations is far beyond any rational need for such defenses. The periodic witch-hunts in which "un-Americans" are ferreted out and exposed as dangers to the nation reveal a deep-seated fear of persons who will not conform to particular sets of national norms.

On the one hand we find in the U.S.A. support for maintaining this nation as the one place on earth which is safe for diversity, while on the other hand we find evidence of great fear of diversity.

7

Exercise

Read and discuss these two selections:

I. Some boys are playing together. One boy says that they should have a race. Another boy, who is smaller than the rest, states that he does not want to run in the race. He starts to walk slowly away from the others, but is stopped by the boy who suggested that they have the race.
What will happen next?

II. A handsome young man works in a place where he sees a beautiful young lady almost every day. He is strong, healthy, and intelligent. He does not have a wife. He would like to marry and have a family. The young lady is graceful, well-mannered, and charming. She too is unmarried.
What will happen next?

Spaceship Survival

If we were not Americans,
what other nationality would we like to be?
What nationality wouldn't we like to be?

Background Reading:

From *Some Dimensions of International Affairs Education* by Paul M. Dietterich.

The person who has atrophied in his affection is suffering from a kind of stunted growth; he has cut off certain segments of the human race from the scope of his concern. He suffers for this by closing himself to a wealth of knowledge and experience that could be his if he were open to other persons and cultures.

Individuals atrophy; nations also atrophy.

Gunnar Myrdal points out that " . . . in none of the existing national cultures are people educated to know and like people in other countries who are different from themselves; on the contrary, they are often indoctrinated with national self-righteousness and are apt to despise, fear, and hate those who are outside the nation and live differently."

Americans, taught that they live in "the land of the free and the home of the brave," and that their nation is first in war and first in the hearts of its countrymen, may be victims of their own educational system and suffer from a built-in parochialism.

A recent worldwide study done by Lambert and Klineberg of children's attitudes toward foreign peoples, in the U.S.A., Bantu children in South Africa, Brazil, Canada, France, Germany, Israel, Japan, Lebanon, and Turkey, should be noted. All children were asked, "If you were not an (American, or Bantu, or Brazilian, etc.) what would you most like to be?"

Children in other countries easily named a number of alternative nationalities, but American children found it difficult to name any other nationality they would like to be.

It may be of interest to note that American children had no difficulty choosing what nationalities they would *not* like to be.

Spaceship Survival Instruction Sheet

A spaceship is traveling around the world and it is seen that the earth is going to be destroyed in one hour. Within that time it is possible for the ship to land ten times to rescue ten people. Your onboard computer has determined that you can find these ten people anywhere in the world.

You are a crew member of the spaceship and you must decide in ten minutes which ten people you will pick up.

Use the following method in making your selections:

Section A lists 22 nationalities and Section B lists 20 professions. Choose a nationality name and write it in front of the person you would want to save, e.g., *Filipino worker*. You may use the same nationality as often as you wish, but you must choose ten different people according to their professions.

Section A:

Japanese	Russian	Indian	English
Nigerian	Brazilian	Australian	Chinese
Canadian	Korean	Italian	Arab
French	South African	Jewish	Indonesian
Peruvian	American (U.S.)	Pakistani	German
	Vietnamese	Filipino	

Section B:

_____	mechanic	_____	peasant
_____	teacher	_____	nurse
_____	police officer	_____	businessman
_____	cook	_____	financier
_____	farmer	_____	soldier
_____	doctor	_____	writer
_____	comedienne	_____	scientist
_____	worker	_____	scholar
_____	minister	_____	maid
_____	housewife	_____	politician

11

Communication—One-Way and Two-Way

Is it worth the effort to do the hard work that open and honest communication demands of us?

Exercise

Use this page and the next to complete the assignment that will be given to you.

Broken Squares

What keeps us from being able to work well with others? On a larger level, what are the obstacles to cooperative development on the part of the peoples and nations of this world?

Exercise

Choose any four letters from the word cooperation *and use them as the initial letters in words that describe elements that are necessary for cooperation among peoples and nations (For example, "T" for "teamwork").*

C –
O –
O –
P –
E –
R –
A –
T –
I –
O –
N –

What is the cartoonist saying about cooperation? What other examples are there of cooperation in this sense?

What's in a Dot?

How do we see the world today and what are our hopes for the future?

Exercise

If one were asked to illustrate the reality of race relations in the United States today using only dots, the picture might look like this: (the collection of dots would suggest polarization).

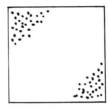

A. How would you use dots to illustrate the reality of the United States today?

B. How would you use dots to illustrate how you think the United States will be in the year 2000?

C. How would you use dots to illustrate how you would like the United States to be in the year 2000?

Time Capsule

Did you ever wonder how the Indians felt about "being discovered" by Columbus?

Exercise

A. Next to each year below list what you consider to be the most meaningful event of that year.

1960 —
1961 —
1962 —
1963 —
1964 —
1965 —
1966 —
1967 —
1968 —
1969 —
1970 —

B. With the help of your parents and other relatives draw up a general outline of your family's history. Include dates of births and deaths, places of origin, travels, and—if possible—any circumstances surrounding events such as immigration to the United States.

List three events that might have been selected by each of the generations in your family as having been the most meaningful events in the world for that period of time.

Call Them as You See Them

How does the world look from the top? How does it appear when you're on the bottom looking up?

Background Reading:

From *Division is the Problem of the Third World* by Julius K. Nyerere, President of Tanzania.

Poverty is not the real problem of the modern world. For we have the knowledge and resources which could enable us to overcome poverty. The real problem—the thing which creates misery, wars and hatred among men—is the division of mankind into rich and poor.

We can see this division at two levels. Within nation states there are a few individuals who have great wealth and whose wealth gives them great power; but the vast majority of people suffer from varying degrees of poverty and deprivation. Even in a country like the United States, this division can be seen. In countries like India, Portugal or Brazil, the contrast between the wealth of a few privileged individuals and the dire poverty of the masses is a crying scandal.

And looking at the world as a collection of nation states, we see the same pattern repeated. There are a few wealthy nations which dominate the world economically, and therefore politically; and a mass of smaller and poor nations whose destiny, it appears, is to be dominated.

The significance about this division between the rich and the poor is not simply that one man has more food than he can eat, more clothes than he can wear and more houses than he can live in, while others are hungry, unclad and homeless. The significant thing about the division between rich and poor nations is not simply that one has the resources to provide comfort for all its citizens, and the other cannot provide basic services.

The reality and depth of the problem arises because the man who is rich has power over the lives of those who are poor, and the rich nation has power over the policies of those who are not rich. And even more important is that our social and economic system, nationally and internationally, supports these divisions and constantly increases them, so that the rich get even richer and more powerful, while the poor get relatively ever poorer and less able to control their own future.

This continues despite all the talk of human equality, the fight against poverty, and of development. Still the rich individuals within nations, and the rich nations within the world, go on getting richer very much faster than the poor overcome their poverty. Sometimes this happens through the deliberate decision of the rich, who use their wealth and their power to that end. But often—perhaps more often—it happens naturally as a result of the normal workings of the social and economic systems men have constructed for themselves.

Just as water from the driest regions of the earth ultimately flows into the oceans where water is already plentiful, so wealth flows from the poorest nations and the poorest individuals into the hands of those nations who are already wealthy. A man who can afford to buy only one loaf of bread a day contributes to the profit accruing to the owner of the bakery, despite the fact that the owner already has more money than he knows how to use. And the poor nation which sells its primary commodities on the world market in order to buy machines for development finds that the prices it obtains, and the prices it has to pay, are both determined by the "forces of the free market" in which it is a pigmy competing with giants.

Both nationally and internationally this division of mankind into the tiny minority of rich and the great majority of poor is rapidly becoming intolerable to the majority—as it should be. The poor nations and the poor peoples of the world are already in rebellion against it; if they do not succeed in securing change which leads towards greater justice, then that rebellion will become an explosion. Injustice and peace are in the long run incompatible!

Instruction Sheet

Below you will find a series of adjectives. Imagine that you are each one of these persons:

1. a coffee worker in El Salvador who slaves all day long in the hot sun to earn $1.44 and who will probably die of "old age" before he is 50;

2. an El Salvadorian *coffee plantation owner* whose income for just *two* years is far greater than the total *lifetime* earnings of one of his coffee workers.

Step 1:

Go through the list of adjectives pretending that you are the *plantation owner* described above. Check off each adjective that you would use to describe one of your coffee workers. Place your checks on the lefthand side of the word. Add other adjectives to the ones listed below, if you'd like.

Step 2:

Go through the list of adjectives again and imagine that you are the *coffee worker* described above. Check off each adjective that you would use to describe the owner of the coffee plantation you work on. Place these checks on the righthand side of the word. Add other adjectives, if you'd like.

intelligent	oppressive	humble	deceptive
shrewd	exploited	childish	arrogant
virtuous	honest	unjust	vengeful
leader	inhuman	creative	skillful
courteous	winner	materialistic	helpful
animal	wise	stupid	cunning
greedy	criminal	honorable	powerful
bloodsucking	pitiless	exploiter	just
communist	lucky	vain	Christian
kind	eager	paternalistic	lazy
well-meaning	misguided	respectful	trustworthy

Why Underdevelopment?

Why are most people in the world poor?
And why are some rich?

Background Reading:

From *Coffee: The Rules of the Game and You* by Thomas P. Fenton.

Juan Diaz is a coffee worker in the Central American Republic of El Salvador. His daily struggle for mere survival is hardly the TV commercial image of life on the hacienda.

Juan and three of his five daughters spend long, hard days in the coffee fields of Montenango. On a good day, Juan picks enough coffee to earn $1.44; and his daughters, a total of $3.35. With $1.24 of these wages, Juan and his wife Paula are able to feed their family for a day. In bad times, Juan and his daughters make as little as 56 cents a day—less than half the money they need just to eat.

At the end of the six-week coffee season, Juan does odd jobs around the hacienda—provided there is work to be done. He can earn about 90 cents there for an eight-hour day. Paula de Diaz supplements her husband's earnings by working in the market. When people have enough money to purchase the tomatoes, cabbages and other homegrown vegetables she sells, Paula can make about 40 cents a day.

The hacienda provides a simple dwelling for the Diaz family, but no modern facilities. Candles are used for light, water has to be hauled from a well and furnishings consist of little more than a table and some chairs. Aside from a dress and shoes for each of the girls during coffee season, the family has not been able to buy much else in the last five years. Whatever money doesn't go for food is spent for visits to the health clinic (40 cents each time), the high interest on bills at the company store, expenses for the children in school and for the burial fee of Juan's father who died last year.

"You know, I look forward to a better life for my children," Juan says. "I dream that if it is possible—if I

21

can possibly afford it—my children will not follow in my footsteps, that they will break out of this terrible way of life. But the money problems we face every day blot out those dreams. I feel bad, nervous, I don't sleep nights worrying about how I'll get something for them to eat. I think and think but don't find any answers. I work hard; my wife and daughters do too. We all do. But still we suffer. Why?"

Many in the past have offered answers to Juan's question. Some say: "He's poor because he's not industrious enough; he's lazy; he's uneducated." Some assert: "He's backward, underdeveloped," perhaps "inferior by nature." Some blame Juan's poverty on an alleged scarcity of natural resources or on the lack of land or modern tools and fertilizers. Some look to the capriciousness of nature—floods, frosts, droughts; and some blame God or fate.

Others place the burden of responsibility for Juan's condition on what may be called the "rules of the game." The "game" encompasses all the national and international systems (economic, political, societal, military) which govern the life of Juan and the development of his country.

Do these rules of the game in fact account for Juan's plight? Examine them and decide for yourself.

What are the rules of the game?

Who makes them? Did Juan or the majority of people in El Salvador play any part in determining them?

How responsible are they for Juan's chronic poverty?

Exercise

Rank these "causes of underdevelopment" in order of importance from #1 to #15. Make note of the ones that you judge to be untrue.

_____ poor land and natural resources

_____ lack of education

_____ international trade policies and practices

_____ feelings of apathy and hopelessness

_____ exploitation and domination by others

_____ the colonial past

_____ the indifference of others

_____ overpopulation

_____ hunger

_____ wealth and power concentrated in the hands of a few

_____ dependency on other countries

_____ no job opportunities

_____ lack of personal initiative

_____ capitalist economic structures

_____ unrest caused by revolutionaries

Charity/Justice

What's the difference?

Exercise

A. *Select what you believe to be the correct answer for each of the following questions:*

1. More than $22 billion worth of American food surpluses has been provided to the less developed countries (LDC's). Of this amount what percentage has been given to them without charge?
   a. less than 25%   b. about 50%   c. all of it

2. Of the following programs, which phase has had the greatest increase in funding by U.S. aid in recent years?
   a. population control   b. Peace Corps   c. contributions to United Nations agencies

3. U.S. aid programs in 1971 spent about $260 million directly in foreign countries. That same year the poor countries paid back to the United States on past loans:
   a. nothing   b. about $100 million   c. more than $300 million

4. Compared to other aid-giving nations, the terms (interest rates and time for repayment) of U.S. government loans to the LDC's are becoming:
   a. tougher   b. easier

5. Of the total Federal Budget, about how much of each $1 is spent for economic aid to the LDC's?
   a. less than $.02   b. about $.50   c. more than $.50

6. Out of each dollar America provides the poor nations for the purchase of goods, how much money actually leaves the U.S.?
   a. less than $.01   b. about $.50   c. more than $.75

7. Which of the following factors accounts for the largest amount of U.S. dollars leaving the country?
   a. defense expenditures   b. foreign aid
   c. private overseas investment   d. American tourists' spending

8. Which accounts for the least amount of U.S. dollars leaving the country?
   a. defense expenditures   b. foreign aid
   c. private overseas investment   d. American tourists' spending

9. The United Nations has set 1% of a nations' wealth (GNP) as a target for ranking the rich nations' contributions to the poor countries. In 1970, out of 16 nations, the U.S. ranked:
   a. 15th   b. 8th   c. 1st

10. Of the total government assistance provided to the poorer nations by the rich nations, the U.S. provides about what percentage?
    a. 40%   b. 60%   c. 80%

11. The cost to each American of the U.S. foreign aid program, including Food for Peace, Peace Corps, etc., is equivalent to:
    a. less than a carton of cigarettes each month
    b. about 10 cartons of cigarettes each month
    c. more than 50 cartons of cigarettes each month.

B. Read and discuss these two selections:

The Rent Strike Model

A social studies teacher in a high school in a poor neighborhood of a major city said: "The students' families live in run-down apartments; their landlords gouge them with high rents; the city officials have a hands-off policy. The best thing I can teach my students is how to conduct a renter's strike. What it is, why it is, how it works—do's and don'ts."

Does this teacher's idea have validity? If not, what are its failings? If valid, does the principle have application in other fields of study?

The Mexico Model

The Synod document (*Justice in the World*) says that the mission of the Church demands that it should courageously denounce injustice. The Mexican hierarchy must be courageous indeed if the statement they released in late 1971 is any indication. In it, the Mexican bishops accuse both the Mexican government and the American citizens of oppressing the Mexican people.

Issued under the direction of Bishop Alfredo Torres of Mexico City, the statement indicts the Mexican government for covering up the dehumanizing conditions of the majority of Mexicans. By describing Mexico as "a paradise, a country of peace and law and of good will," the government entices tourist dollars and foreign investment, "and thus maintains present conditions and dependency." The United States was charged with making Mexico "a mere subsidiary of the American system."

Even more remarkable in its candor is the Mexican bishops' self-condemnation. The statement noted that, historically, "pomp and angelic aloofness has placed the Church on the side of the oppressors."

In speaking of "the side of the oppressors," the statement of the Mexican hierarchy highlights the fact that the pursuit of justice places the Church in the context of two power blocs: one, the presently powerful; the other, the potentially powerful, the presently powerless. The powerful are active through a network of numerous forces and influences operating to maintain the existing system. This bloc considers that justice is already a reality, to be maintained by a system of law and order.

The potentially powerful bloc is comprised of the atomized and disparate groups of people for whom justice is not a reality; it is only an aspiration. A compelling sense of justice provides the impetus and the dynamism for their struggle for liberation.

The Church in pursuit of justice will necessarily confront the powerful, since it is not in the self-interest of this bloc that efforts to achieve justice for the powerless be successful. To pursue justice requires innovations that cut deeply into the existing order.

For this reason, the institutional Church's efforts in the field of justice have tended to be short-lived. As the Church probes into the power structure, pressure from the active bloc mounts, and tends to deflect the Church's efforts into the more traditional and less controversial mode of ministering in charity to the needy. Old slogans reemerge, like: "The Church is a friend of the poor," and "The poor we shall always have with us."

The power bloc is quite ready to support the Church in its humanitarian programs. The U.S. federal tax structure, for example, allows annual corporation deductions for charitable contributions in the amount of $5 billion. The fact that businesses contribute only about one-fifth of their allowable deductions perhaps only serves to highlight the fact that, not only is the achieving of justice for the powerless not a high priority for a major sector of the active power bloc, but charity is not one of their dominant concerns either.

In the accommodation the Church makes with the active-power bloc, in which acts of charity begin to replace the pursuit of justice, the powerless are not forgotten, lest in their alienation and frustration they become a threat to the existing structures. The powerless become the recipients of the powerful's "contribution—deductible for income tax purposes." And for those who are hungry and destitute, unemployed and alienated, a handout of food or clothing is more real than the rhetoric of liberals who merely talk about justice.

However, because of the Church's public statements about justice, the poor are led to believe that injustices can and will be eradicated. Not only is the Church's credibility put on the line, but, more importantly, the hopes and expectations of the powerless are raised.

Sixty years ago, Mexico was wrenched by revolution, and the Church was a target of the landless rebels because it was identified with the rich and powerful. Today the institutional Church in Mexico is attempting to make a break with its reactionary past. What is not clear about this move, as well as similar efforts elsewhere, are the consequences for the Church of identifying itself so clearly with the needs, in justice, of the oppressed.

Letter to Pepe

How do we feel about things like violence, revolutionary change, and socialism?

Background Reading:

From *Can the United States Promote Foreign Development?*
by Richard J. Barnet

There is even less validity to the counterinsurgency rationale for military aid. U.S. policies now keep in power many governments which, if concerned about development at all, are committed to superimposing an extremely narrow "developed" economy and social structure on top of a deteriorating traditional society. Such governments must rule by fear and the U.S. gives them the means to do it. It is likely to advance the development process whenever such governments fall.

The U.S. should abandon its present bias which holds that a repressive "capitalist" government is better than any insurgent or revolutionary government or better than the "chaos" that would follow the overthrow of the many regimes that now survive only with massive American aid. (If aid were withdrawn those regimes that were flexible enough to win popular support would survive. The rest would fall.) Disorder and revolution may be a necessary stage of development for many countries and the U.S. should learn to live with them. A repressive order which perpetuates conditions of acute misery is not clearly preferable. The U.S. does not need to "promote revolution" as a few enthusiastic rhetoricians among American political figures have suggested. Such a policy would be inconsistent with the requirements of international law and traditional diplomacy. What is needed is to stop supporting counterrevolution. Robert Heilbroner has correctly indicated that "our present policy prefers the absence of development to the chance for Communism—which is to say that we prefer hunger and want and the existing inadequate assaults against the causes of hunger and want to any regime that declares its hostility to capitalism." Military assistance and supporting assistance designed to release local funds for military

29

and police purposes are an investment in counterrevolution and an obstacle to development.

If the U.S. were to make development a serious goal, it would support development efforts of revolutionary governments rather than harass them. Any government that can mobilize the populations of traditional societies to make the achievements in health, literacy, and food production and distribution that have been made in Cuba, North Vietnam, and China should be applauded, not blockaded, boycotted, or bombed. It is clear that no country or ideology has the answer to the problems of development. Certainly the American experience, with all its success, has limited relevance to primitive economies. If there is to be hope of survival, many competing ideas and models of development will have to be tried. What will work in one country or region may not work in another. The present bias in U.S. development policy in favor of private enterprise and against socialism forecloses desperately needed possibilities and forces destructive choices on poor governments. The U.S. should encourage all development efforts and should not discriminate against revolutionary governments or socialist experiments. As long as the U.S. views the successes of revolutionary governments as foreign policy defeats, we will continue to be an enemy of development.

That the U.S. should take satisfaction from, and in some cases contribute to, crop failures in Cuba, Vietnam, or China is eloquent testimony of our real concern with the misery of underdevelopment. Here again the U.S. could make a great contribution to development by stopping destructive policies. It should no longer be the policy of the United States to complicate the life of revolutionary regimes through military harrassment and economic warfare. It should be noted that these policies directly encourage those repressive features of revolutionary regimes we say we find offensive. Since the allied intervention at the time of the bolshevik revolution, "capitalist encirclement" has been used by revolutionary regimes to justify harrrassment of internal opposition and police repression. Blockades, overflights, and invasions do not encourage governments to deal more kindly with their own populations. A government under external attack will become increasingly repressive.

Exercise

A foreign student you met last summer has returned to his home in Latin America. You receive the following letter from him. How would you reply?

My dear friend,

As you know, I went to the United States with great hopes. I expected to find there students who would understand the tragedy and agony of my people and who would be anxious to encourage and help us as we try to solve our problems. But I returned home sadly disillusioned. I am convinced now that most people in the United States have no idea of the social revolution we are caught up in today. They seem, too, to have little interest in learning about it.

I have heard people in your country talk about the freedoms they want us to have; no one seemed much concerned about the injustice we can no longer bear. Many North Americans have some vague knowledge that my people are hungry, ill-clad, in poor health, and living in extreme poverty. But they don't seem to know why—and they don't seem to care enough to want to do something about it.

But since you are my friend, I am writing to you to let you know that I have joined the Frente de Liberación Nacional. Our goal is to overthrow the repressive dictatorship which has gained so much support from the capitalists here and overseas and which continues to exploit the majority of my people. We hope we can do this without bloodshed, but *we will do it.*

Already we are planning how to govern the country when the revolution is achieved. Our government will be democratic and socialist. We will need the support of other socialist countries—and of friends like yourself.

Specifically, my dear friend, I have a request to make of you. Our FLN forces are engaged in grassroots education and health care with the peasants. We need money to purchase supplies. Can you help? I assure you that any money you send will *not* be used for the purchase of the weapons we need.

What do you say, my friend? Remember I told you it might come to this. Many in your country will not understand and will be against us. How about you?

If you can help us financially, I will send you further instructions. Please write.

Your brother,

Pepe

31

On Trial: An American War

What do we believe about war and peace?

Program Notes

To kill another human being is clearly a violation of God's law. But are there circumstances when it is not sinful to take the life of another person? In particular, is it possible that warfare, during which persons are killed on a massive scale, is not only tolerable, but just, and therefore morally lawful?

As the early Christians began to take an ever larger role in the affairs of civil society, these questions became the subject of grave pastoral concern for Churchmen. Saint Augustine, in the fourth century, began to attempt to deal with the issue. Of all the rationales that societies have constructed to evaluate the justness of warfare, the theory which Saint Augustine began to develop has received the widest treatment. It is known as the Just War Theory, and some of the greatest names in Catholic theology and ethics have contributed to it—Thomas Aquinas, Francisco de Vittoria, Francisco Suarez.

Over the centuries, these men have elaborated criteria which must be strictly adhered to in order for a war to be just. Before a nation can resort to war, the theory requires that the nation must have a just cause; only the nation's competent and appropriate authority can make the official decision that war is required in the national interest; and the nation must follow the principle of proportionality in conducting the war.

The initial Just War criterion of "just cause" states that the nation must be suffering a real and grave wrong perpetrated by the offending nation(s), and this wrong is so serious that it must be righted. It is this criterion of the Just War Theory—the nation's "just cause"—that is explored in the playlet "On Trial: An American War."

33

"On Trial" is not a Joe McCarthy-type witch-hunt; nor is it modeled after the Nuremberg trials. It does not seek to convict persons for violations of the international laws of war. It is the moral dimension of war that is examined. The playlet, therefore, tries to place a war on trial, not the personalities alive at the time. The essential question it raises is: Did the United States have a "just cause" to declare war on Spain in 1898?

This is the explicit issue for trial. However, "trials" on other levels are implicit here. And St. Augustine, the judge in the trial, raises some of these in his summation and charge to the members of the jury—the audience.

More fundamentally, however, the Just War Theory itself is "on trial." Can the Theory, in fact, be used to judge the justness or morality of a war? Perhaps, as John Courtney Murray, S.J., an eminent Catholic moralist of the 1960's said, in speaking of Christians' failure to apply the Just War principles to the fire bombing of Dresden, Hamburg, and Tokyo: " . . . the traditional doctrine was irrelevant during World War II . . . . But there is a place for an indictment of all of us who failed to make the traditional doctrine relevant." Or, perhaps, as pacifists have always concluded, the Just War Theory compromises the Gospel message about the sacredness of all human life and allows the Gospel to be manipulated to serve the purposes of nation-states.

To be any good, a theory has to be useful. "On Trial: An American War" examines the practicality of the Just War Theory. If practical, the theory can be applied to a particular past war. This can assist citizens to examine their nation's history, and to understand its implications for the present. This is the ongoing "trial."

The Cast

Judge:
  St. Augustine

Witnesses:
  John Data
  Charles Footnote

Lawyers:
  Defender
  Prosecutor

Jury:
  The Audience

NOTE: Do *not* read this script until after the play has been performed.

SCRIPT
ON TRIAL: AN AMERICAN WAR

ST. A   I'm not Saint Augustine. I know your Program Notes say I am. But God knows I'm no saint, and so do you. I'm just standing in for Augustine—to represent him and a number of other greats whose names are in your Program: men like Aquinas, de Vittoria and Suarez. These men, over the years, worked out the doctrine we call the Just War Theory. (*Making a hand gesture to the posterboard at the center back of stage*) You see here a listing of the requirements for a war to be just. Today, we're going to apply one of the principles of this theory to a real war. That principle is the one circled—the just cause.

   The Just War Theory requires that, before a nation can go to war, it must have a just cause for doing so. The nation must have suffered, or be suffering, a real and grave wrong; and that wrong is so severe that it must be righted. The question before you, as members of the jury, is this: Did the United States meet that just cause requirement when it declared war against Spain in 1898? To decide this issue the court will now hear testimony.

(*Defense lawyer walks to the lawyer reading stand.*)

DEF   The defense is prepared to demonstrate that the action the United States was forced to take against Spain fully met the standard criterion of just cause as defined in the Just War Theory. I call Mr. John Data to the witness stand.

(*John Data walks to the witness reading stand.*)

DEF   Please give your name and your occupation.

JD   My name is John Data. I'm a U.S. citizen and a compiler of information about the Spanish-American War.

DEF   Would you sketch for us the background leading up to the war?

JD   The general attitude of most Americans toward Europe during the 1800's is very significant. Americans were skeptical and cautious about the intrigues of Europeans and their continual squabbles.

This attitude toward Europe is evident in two official U.S. documents.

DEF   What are these documents, Mr. Data?

JD   Washington's Farewell Address and the Monroe Doctrine.

DEF   Your honor, I would like to place these documents in the record as Exhibits A and B.

ST. A   First, let's see what relevance they have to the Spanish-American War. Mr. Data, would you summarize the highpoints of these documents?

JD   Yes, Your Honor, I'd be glad to. Washington gave his Farewell Address in 1796. At that time, the United States was young, and relatively weak. President Washington spoke mainly about America's foreign policy. He said—and I'm reading from his Address—quote: Europe has interests which are very different from ours. She, therefore, becomes engaged in frequent controversies and wars. Why should we entangle our peace and prosperity in Europe's ambitions and rivalries. If we remain a united and efficient people, the period is not far off when we will be in command of our own future. Our policy, Washington said, is to steer clear of permanent alliances with any part of the foreign world. End of quote.

ST. A   What about the other document—the Monroe Doctrine?

JD   If I may, I'd like to read an excerpt which sums up President Monroe's message to Congress in 1823: No part of the American continents is to be considered as available for future colonization by European nations. We should consider any attempt by Europeans to extend their system to any part of Latin America as dangerous to the peace and safety of the United States.

DEF   Your Honor, these official statements document the position that the United States had a policy of non-intervention in European affairs.

ST. A   They seem to be relevant. You may place them in the record as Exhibits A and B.

DEF   Thank you, Your Honor.

(*DEF takes two large envelopes, walks to the small table at center stage, places the envelopes on the table and returns to the lawyer reading stand.*)

DEF   Mr. Data, what finally led up to the war between the United States and Spain in 1898?

JD   The Cuban situation. Cuba was part of the colonial empire of Spain, and had been since the time of Columbus. In the mid-1800's, the Cubans unsuccessfully attempted to revolt against Spain, and the war lasted about ten years. In 1895, under the leadership of the Cuban patriot José Martí, another war of independence broke out. This time, the rebels engaged in successful guerrilla warfare against the Spanish troops stationed on the island.

DEF   How did Spain react?

JD   They sent General Campos to command the Spanish Army in Cuba. Campos had put down the Cuban revolution 20 years before. But the new insurrection had wider popular support, and he was unable to defeat the revolutionaries. In less than a year, the rebels secured much of the island and they were on the outskirts of the capital city, Havana.

DEF   In other words, Mr. Data, the island had been in a state of chronic violence and repeated uprisings for a number of years.

JD   That's correct.

DEF   What was the official U.S. reaction?

JD   It was cautious and restrained.

DEF   Would you elaborate on that?

JD   The United States assured Spain that it had no designs on Cuba, and that it was interested in cooperating with Spain in the immediate pacification of the island. However, the Spanish government was reminded that U.S. investments and properties, like sugar refineries and railroads, were being damaged. President Cleveland offered his assistance to help arrange a peaceful settlement. His plan, he said, would maintain Spain's sovereignty over the island, but also would provide a reasonable degree of local self-government for the Cubans.

DEF   In view of the success of the Cuban rebels and the concern expressed by the United States, did the Spanish government change its tactics?

JD   Only in that it increased its military force. Campos was relieved of his command and replaced by General Weyler. Several hundred thousand additional troops were sent to the island. Since the revolutionaries were aided by the peasants in the rural areas, Weyler decided to remove the peasants from the countryside. Hundreds of thousands of Cubans were forced from their homes and herded into campsites in the towns and cities.

DEF   Did the people in the United States know what was happening?

JD   Yes. The U.S. observer on the scene described the dehumanizing conditions in the concentration camps as gruesome. He felt the policy would result in the extinction of the Cuban people. The American consul in Havana estimated that by the end of 1897, some two hundred thousand Cubans had died in the camps and another two hundred thousand were dying of starvation. In spite of these tactics, the Cuban patriots persisted in their rebellion.

DEF   How did these tactics affect the United States?

JD   In December 1896, almost two years after the revolution began, President Cleveland repeated his desire to see—what he termed—the pacification of the island. The President pointed out that America's concern was by no means only humanitarian. He reminded the Spanish government that Americans had millions of dollars invested in Cuba, and that, before the outbreak of violence, our volume of trade with the island had been substantial.

DEF   Did Cleveland say anything about how the American people felt about the revolution?

JD   Yes. He told Spain that a number of Americans were demanding some sort of intervention on the part of the United States. And he warned Spain that if it could not control the Cuban situation, the United States might be forced to take some positive action.

DEF   William McKinley was inaugurated President in the following year, 1897. What was his attitude toward the Cuban affair?

JD   In his Inaugural Address, McKinley stressed America's continuing interest in opening up new markets for our products. Let us move out, he said, to new fields and increase the sale of our products in foreign markets. Our only purpose is to open trade wherever we can. He also said, We want no wars of conquest. We resist the temptation of European empires to grab colonial possessions. He did not mention Cuba by name.

DEF   If he didn't mention Cuba in his Inaugural Address, how did he inform Spain of his views on the Cuban situation?

JD   He appointed a new Ambassador to Spain, Stewart Woodford, and gave him specific instructions.

DEF   What were these instructions?

JD   First, McKinley told Woodford how he saw the situation. McKinley said, quote: The extraordinary interest of the United States in

38

the Cuban situation cannot be ignored. Our citizens are greatly concerned about their property and commercial ventures in Cuba. The chronic conditions of trouble and violence in Cuba constantly cause social and political unrest in the United States. And these continuous irritations injure the normal function of business and delay the condition of prosperity to which America is entitled. End of quote.

DEF   That was background for Woodford. What was he supposed to tell Spain?

JD   Mainly two things. As McKinley put it: Our sincere wish is to give aid to Spain in order that an enduring peace may result. However, McKinley also added: The United States has a moral obligation under international law to wait only a reasonable time for Spain to settle the Cuban uprising, and the limits of our endurance have just about been reached. Woodford was specifically instructed, according to the document, to bring this matter to the attention of the Spanish government with all the earnestness which the constantly imperiled national interests of the United States justify. And Woodford did exactly that.

DEF   Your Honor, I would like to place these instructions in the record.

ST. A   You may place them in the record as Exhibit C.

(*DEF takes third large envelope to small table in center stage, places it on the table and returns to the lawyer reading stand.*)

DEF   Thank you, Mr. Data.

ST. A   The witness may step down.

(*JD leaves the witness reading stand and returns to chair 3 as DEF continues reading.*)

DEF   Your Honor, from the evidence just presented, it is clear that the United States, in the 1800's, had a policy of non-intervention in the affairs of European nations. Secondly, it had exercised great self-restraint in the Cuban affair. However, the chronic violence that characterized that island was both a continuous hazard and the cause of serious injury to the United States. Finally, since Spain was incapable of solving the problem, the United States was justified in taking positive action to do so. Your Honor, the defense rests its case.

39

ST. A   Thank you. The Court will now hear the case for the prosecution.

(*DEF returns to chair 4; the lawyer for the prosecution walks to the lawyer reading stand.*)

PRO   Your Honor, the prosecution is prepared to show that the United States did not meet the just cause criterion of the Just War Theory. Rather, the United States went to war against Spain to satisfy its own very narrowly defined self-interests. During the years preceding the Spanish-American War, the United States was continually expanding its commercial interests overseas. As a consequence, the United States was frequently involved in military skirmishes, and finally, by 1898, in a full-scale war. I call Mr. Charles Footnote to the stand.

(*Charles Footnote walks to the witness reading stand.*)

PRO   Would you please give your name and occupation?

CF   My name is Charles Footnote. I'm a U.S. citizen and a compiler of information about the Spanish-American War.

PRO   Mr. Footnote, do you take issue with the facts as they have been presented?

CF   No, sir. As far as the defense counsel chose to present them, they were substantially correct.

PRO   How do you mean, as far as the defense counsel chose to present them? Is there additional information that should be presented?

CF   I'd say so, definitely. In the first place, it's correct to say, as Mr. Data did, that the United States adopted a general policy of non-intervention in the affairs of Europe in the early 1800's. But that's only part of the story. After the Civil War in the mid-1800's, the United States began to expand its trade and commercial interests. At the same time, the United States found it necessary to increase its military power.

PRO   Its military power, Mr. Footnote?

CF   Yes, particularly the navy. Ten years before we declared war on Spain, the Secretary of the Navy argued: The nation that is ready to strike the first blow will gain an advantage which its enemy can never offset. He predicted that future U.S. naval action would be necessary in the Gulf of Mexico and the Pacific Ocean. He said American interests there were growing rapidly and were too imperiled, quote, to be left unprotected, unquote. By 1895, the

American navy had moved from twelfth to seventh place among the navies of the world.

PRO   What were the American interests that needed the navy's protection?

CF   Chiefly its expanding business interests in cotton goods, bananas, sugar, oil and railroads. And these interests were primarily in Latin America and in China. During the period in question, the United States took armed actions against other nations on 29 occasions, 28 of them in Latin America and the Pacific. That shows a definite relationship between economic interests and military power.

DEF   (*standing*) Objection. Your Honor, the prosecution is suggesting that the United States was roaming the high seas, intent on building an empire. Is is not true, Mr. Footnote, that these military actions were taken to protect the lives and property of American citizens?

CF   That's precisely the point. The United States was becoming a commercial world power and a policy of non-intervention was no longer consistent with these interests.

(*DEF sits down.*)

PRO   The United States had a particular interest in China at this time, is that not correct, Mr. Footnote?

DEF   (*standing*) Your Honor, I object to this whole line of questioning. The U.S. declaration of war against Spain specifically referred to Cuba. There wasn't even a mention of the Pacific area in that document, much less of China.

PRO   Your Honor, the prosecution is prepared to show the relevance of the U.S.-China relationship to the issue before the court.

ST. A   Proceed, Mr. Footnote.

(*DEF sits down.*)

CF   In 1898, after declaring war on Spain, the United States invaded the Philippine Islands. The Philippines, like Cuba, were part of Spain's colonial empire. The United States eventually took over the islands completely. To understand why, we have to look at the growing relationship between the United States and China.
      The United States signed its first trade agreement with China in 1844. By 1889, the U.S. consul at Peking reported that China is a

41

vast market for commerce not sufficiently exploited. However, he warned American businessmen that foreigners hold their place in China by military force and by force alone.

PRO   Did the United States develop its trade with China?

CF   Yes, it did. During the 1890's our trade with China doubled, and it seemed likely to continue. However, the other major commercial nations—Great Britain, France and Germany—began to carve up the China market, and American businessmen feared these nations would block the United States out of China. They pressured McKinley to take steps to defend our treaty rights and protect our commercial interests in China.

ST. A   Mr. Footnote, how is this relevant to the cause of the Spanish-American War?

CF   I'm coming to that, Your Honor. Theodore Roosevelt was the Assistant Secretary of the Navy at the time and he felt that war with Spain was very likely. He pressed upon McKinley a comprehensive plan of action in the Pacific in the event of war. Among other things, he advised—and I'm quoting Roosevelt here—Our Asiatic squadron should blockade, and if possible, take Manila, the capital of the Philippines.

PRO   Did McKinley authorize any military action in the Philippines?

CF   Yes. Eleven days after declaring war on Spain, Dewey sailed into Manila Bay and destroyed Spain's Asiatic fleet. *The Wall Street Journal* was saying, at the time, that the U.S. should retain interest in the Philippines to protect not only existing trade with the East, but the greater trade likely to be developed. Over the next three years, the United States sent more than one hundred thousand troops to the Philippines, fighting Filipinos to gain undisputed possession of the islands.

PRO   *(Goes to the easel and turns posterboard around so that the map faces the audience.)* Your Honor, the prosecution offers as Exhibit 1 this map showing the location of the 28 armed actions taken by the United States. This is an average of one intervention every 15 months. *(PRO goes back to lawyer reading stand and continues reading.)* I offer this as ample proof that the U.S. policy was not one of non-intervention, but rather, one of intervention when its interests conflicted with those of other nations. The defense suggests that the U.S. action was characterized by self-restraint. I suggest, rather, that it was the self-restraint of the nations against whom the actions were taken that presented escalation of any of these actions into full-scale war.

With reference to Cuba, the Defense would have us believe that

U.S. interests were severely imperiled by the Cuban situation. Mr. Footnote, what were the facts?

CF   The fact is that Americans had about one and a half billion dollars invested in foreign countries. Less than 6% of that was invested in Cuba. Our trade with Cuba was also a relatively small part of our total world trade, less than 6%. This is not to say that some Americans were not adversely affected by events in Cuba. They were, but that group was relatively small, although quite influential.

PRO   Thank you, Mr. Footnote.

ST. A   The witness may step down.

(CF leaves the witness reading stand and returns to chair 1 as PRO continues reading.)

PRO   Your Honor, I submit that the cause for which the United States declared war against Spain was insufficient to satisfy the requirements of the just cause criterion. Therefore, the United States was involved in an unjust war with Spain, with Cuba and with the Philippines. Your Honor, the prosecution rests its case.

ST. A   Thank you. Does the defense have concluding remarks?

DEF   Yes, I do.

(DEF walks to lawyer reading stand; PRO returns to chair 2.)

DEF   Your Honor, there is no question that the events leading up to the war against Spain were complex and fast-moving. However, the United States had no intention to acquire the Philippine Islands when it went to war against Spain. These islands were simply thrust upon us by fate. This is very clear in the words of President McKinley: The truth is, I didn't want the Philippines, and when they came to us as a gift from the gods, I didn't know what to do with them. When the Spanish War broke out, I ordered Dewey to go to Manila and capture or destroy the Spanish fleet. But that was as far as I thought. Then, however, there was nothing for us to do but to take the Philippine Islands, and, McKinley said, educate, uplift and Christianize the Filipinos. End of quote.
       But, Your Honor, let us focus on the real issue in this case. The fact is, the United States went to war with Spain to bring peace to Cuba. The Spanish troops were unable to put down the uprising;

43

and the rebels were unable to defeat Spain. Neither side could resolve the turmoil. The island was in chaos. The United States had to intervene. Therefore, I request the jury to find that the United States' cause for declaring war was just.

ST. A   Thank you. Does the Prosecution have concluding remarks?

PRO   Yes, I do.

(PRO walks to lawyer reading stand; DEF returns to chair 4.)

PRO   Your Honor, a nation's cause for going to war is just when that nation is suffering a wrong so severe it must be righted. To suggest that events in Cuba occasioned anything more than irritation for the United States is a gross exaggeration. To suggest that the Philippines posed a threat is absurd.

The defense claims the United States went to war to bring peace to Cuba. That isn't how the Cubans viewed the situation. Writing in the early days of the Cuban revolt, José Martí who led the Cuban uprising and gave his life in that effort, said:

Let my words express the weariness of an oppressed people who hope through their struggle to achieve a government of their own. Cuba must be free both from Spain and from the United States. The hour is fast approaching when America might go so far as to intervene. We do not want to remove the present oppression only to find that the old colonial spirit returns in the new dress of a Yankee uniform. This is our war. This is the Republic of Cuba we are creating. All I have done and shall ever do, Martí said, is fight for Cuba's independence. End of quote.

Your Honor, the subsequent events proved that Martí's fears were justified. After the declaration of war against Spain, U.S. troops invaded Cuba and occupied the island for virtually all of the next 25 years. The United States simply replaced Spain as the dominant colonial power. Therefore, I request the jury to find the United States guilty of perpetrating an unjust war.

ST. A   Thank you.

(PRO returns to chair 2 as St. A continues reading, directing his remarks to the audience.)

ST. A   Both the defense and the prosecution have presented their cases. It is now up to you, ladies and gentlemen of the jury, to decide the issue.

It is important to recall that, in this case, the two major

powers—the United States and Spain—did not pose immediate and direct threats to each other. Neither nation had plans to attack the home ports or coastlines of the other. Both countries, rather, focused exclusively on conditions of conflict in offshore islands —Cuba and the Philippines.

It is also necessary to note that a people's struggle for independence from colonial domination frequently results in violence and instability in that colony. More powerful nations often exploit these conditions to satisfy their own selfish interests. When they do so, they violate the principles of justice.

The verdict depends on you. As the jury, you must decide. On one level, the question before you is this: Since the United States initiated the action of officially declaring war against Spain, did the United States have a just cause for going to war? That is, was the United States suffering a real and grave wrong, a wrong so severe that it had to be righted? If it was not, you must find the U.S. government guilty of violating the traditional Christian doctrine of just war.

On another level, Spain is on trial. Was the Spanish government guilty of unjustly suppressing the people of Cuba by resisting the Cuban movement for independence?

On yet a third level, there are the actions of the Cuban people themselves. During the 1800's, Cubans repeatedly rebelled against Spanish authority. Were they guilty of injustice in breaking the laws and disrupting the order established by the Spanish government?

For the purpose of making your determination, only the evidence presented in the trial is to be used. Data acquired from other sources are not allowable in your deliberation. The case, then, is in your hands. Was there a violation of the just cause principle of the Just War Theory? If so, who is guilty? Who is innocent?

What is your verdict?

(*ST. A and the other readers walk off the stage.*)

END

Every Man My Brother?

Why do people discriminate against one another?

NOTE: Do *not* read this script until after the play has been performed.

SCRIPT
EVERY MAN MY BROTHER
PART ONE

(CANDOR comes to his reading stand from seat in audience. Begins to read.)

CANDOR Candor's my name. Henry J. Candor. I'm an eye doctor. I've been fitting people with glasses since 'way before the last war. Funny thing about people. Sometimes they'd rather squint than wear glasses. But testing people's eyes can be a tricky business. When I ask a person to look at an eye chart and say, "Read line 3," if they can't see it, some get mad at me. All I did was ask them to look. And I guess that's what I'm doing here now—trying to provide a better look at some colors, like red, black, brown and white.

(CANDOR moves to easel. Removes eye chart, places it face down on the small table. Returns to reading stand. FIRST and SECOND READERS come to their reading stands from seats in the audience as CANDOR continues to read.)

CANDOR The first color on the chart is red. Red is the color of rage, and fire, and blood, and the American Indian. Maybe a good place to start looking at the color red is Wounded Knee Creek: December 29, 1890.

FIRST READER Soldiers of the U.S. Cavalry surround the remnants of the Sioux Indians just west of Wounded Knee Creek in South Dakota. Soldiers are stationed on all sides of the camp. Four Hotchkiss guns are posted on a slight hill and trained directly on the camp. Some of the soldiers search the tepees for weapons. They overturn beds, shoving aside the Indian women who protest loudly and try to bar their way. Most of the Sioux men have knives under their blankets and are becoming agitated by the cries of their women.

SECOND READER The soldiers find about forty guns. A young brave, who is concealing a gun under his blanket, pulls out the gun and fires, killing one of the soldiers.

The troops respond instantly with a volley of rifle fire at point-blank range, killing about half of the Indians. The rest of the Sioux throw off their blankets and draw their knives or pull out old-fashioned war clubs and grapple with the soldiers. The Hotchkiss guns then fire into the camp. The rest of the troops begin shooting at the Indians attempting to flee. Within minutes, more than three hundred Indian men, women and children are killed.

CANDOR   Members of the U.S. cavalry gave eye-witness accounts.

(THIRD READER rises and faces the audience.)

THIRD READER   It made me sick to look at the awful sight. A girl, about eighteen, was lying on the ground supporting herself on her hand, the blood spurting from her mouth. Near her lay two other Indians, and all around, like patches on the snow, were dead squaws, each in a pool of blood. We found a baby who was unhurt, but the mother was dead. She must have been shot with a revolver held not five feet away. Her hair was burned and her skin blackened with powder burns.

(THIRD READER sits down.)

CANDOR   So that ended it. Near Wounded Knee Creek in South Dakota, a hungry and defeated band of Sioux was goaded and frightened into making a gesture of resistance against the United States Cavalry. The Indian wars had ended, and with it an era also ended, in which all American Indians, from the Atlantic Ocean to the Pacific, had tried to preserve their ancestral lands and their cultural ways.

FOURTH READER *(remaining seated)*   Why don't we go back to the beginning, back when it all started?

CANDOR   It may not be possible for us to see the real red man, the authentic face of the American Indian. We have seen him distorted so often in movies and TV Westerns. But we do have an observer of that early scene, back before the wagon trains and massacres. Christopher Columbus tells us about the Indians that he first met.

FIRST READER   I believe that I must have come to the garden of a New Eden. The Indians are so entirely our friends. Anything they have, if asked for it, they give to us. They show us so much lovingness as though they would give us their hearts.

CANDOR   At first, the Indians warmly welcomed the Europeans as visitors. In 1607, Powhatan, chief of the Indians in Virginia, greeted Captain John Smith:

SECOND READER   Do not come with your guns and swords to invade us. What good will it do for you to take by force that which you may peacefully have with our love: Rest well, and sleep peacefully in the midst of our women and children.

48

CANDOR   A source of conflict between the Indians and the white settlers was the attitude about land.

SECOND READER   For the Indian, land had a deeply religious significance. He treated the land just like he treated the people around him. He wanted to live there and let others live there also. The Indian did not understand the "value" of land in white man's terms, that is, as a piece of property for speculation.

CANDOR   The clash over the two views of land value led to a clash over the possession of the land itself. The white man wanted the Indian to quit being Indian, give up his Indian customs, and start acting like a white man. It was that simple. Oh, there was just one more thing. The white man also wanted the land, and that's where the trouble started.

FOURTH READER *(remaining seated)*   That's right. When Columbus first arrived here the place was owned by Indians, over two billion acres stretching from the Atlantic to the Pacific Ocean. How did they lose it?

FIRST READER   It was not because the white men were "savages" any more than the Indians were that the wars between the two were so cruel. These wars did not consist of battles fought by the armies of nations. On the one side were the armies from Europe, and later the United States. But on the other side was the whole of the Indian people—men, women, and children—desperately defending their homes.

(THIRD READER rises and faces the audience.)

CANDOR   The white men seemed to be appalled at the fierce resistance they met when they invaded the Indians' land. They called the Indians "savages." For example, the American Declaration of Independence speaks of the Indians as:

THIRD READER   merciless Indian Savages, whose known rule of warfare is an undistinguished destruction of all ages, sexes, and conditions.

CANDOR   General George Custer:

THIRD READER   The Indian is savage in every sense of the word and has a cruel, ferocious nature.

(THIRD READER sits down.)

CANDOR   Another tone that developed during these years was that not only is the color red bad, but red is better dead. Introducing himself to General Philip Sheridan, a Comanche added, "Me good Indian." Sheridan replied:

FIRST READER   The only good Indians I know are dead.

CANDOR   With such bitterness between whites and reds, it is little wonder that atrocities occurred.

FIRST READER   In 1779, General George Washington sent troops to pacify some Iroquois who had been harassing white settlers in Pennsylvania and New York. General John Sullivan led the attack, and scores of Indian homes were burnt out. Little resistance was encountered from the Indians who retreated to the shelter of British posts, but not all escaped. Some Indians were killed and their bodies flayed to provide boot tops for the soldiers.

SECOND READER   In 1830, President Andrew Jackson ordered the forced removal of all Indian tribes east of the Mississippi River. During the next ten years, an estimated 80,000 Indians were herded westward, across the Mississippi. Thousands died from disease and starvation on the thousand-mile forced march.

CANDOR   In 1849, gold was discovered in California.

SECOND READER   The gold rush attracted thousands of whites who inundated the Indians' land in California, destroying their villages and overrunning their hunting grounds. In time, white attitudes hardened against Indians so that no excuse was needed for hostility against them. Indian children were murdered, and Indian women were raped, or killed indiscriminately. Many Indian adult males were rounded up for slave labor.

CANDOR   So that's what red looks like. Indians once owned two billion acres of land. Today they have 50 million acres—about the size of New England, less than 3% of the land they started with.
So I guess that's it for the color red.

FOURTH READER   Not quite!

(FOURTH READER rises, walks up to the easel, looks at the chart, then turns to the audience and reads.)

FOURTH READER   There are several more shades to the color red which must never be forgotten. We Indians have been here for thousands of years. This is our homeland.
We have our own distinctive cultures, and we have different points of view from those that come from Western European and Judeo-Christian traditions.
We are the only people in America who have been militarily conquered. But we are living proof that no people has ever been forced by another group into forsaking its own culture.

(FOURTH READER returns to his seat in audience.)

50

PART TWO

(CANDOR walks to easel. Removes red chart, places it face down on table. Returns to reading stand.)

CANDOR   The next color is black. Black is the color of shoe polish, and darkness, and despair—and the American Negro. *(Pause)* It all started simply enough, the business of buying and selling black men. Not that America invented the slave trade, it had been going on for a long time. According to John Rolfe, an early colonist, it happened this way:

FIRST READER   Toward the end of August 1619, a Dutch warship arrived at a port in the Virginia Colony. Its only cargo was 20 Negroes which Governor Berkeley acquired by trading food supplies.

CANDOR   That was it. America was in the slave business. John Barbot *(pronounced Bar-bo)*, a slave merchant of those early days, describes a typical scene at a port city on the West Coast of Africa where the slave ships started out.

SECOND READER   After the round-up, blacks were put in corrals on the beach. They were then brought out naked into a large area where doctors examined them and separated the healthy ones from the weak. Slave dealers then began the bidding. When a black had been purchased, he was immediately branded with a red-hot iron.

FIRST READER   Each company had its own branding spot, such as the cheek or the arm. After a place on the skin was rubbed with grease and a piece of oil paper put over it, the branding iron was pressed against the skin. The skin swelled painfully and at once the letters became visible, and remained so forever.

CANDOR   The trip across the Atlantic was a brutal experience.

SECOND READER   Slaves were packed like coffins on shelves in the hold of the slave ships. The shelves were often separated by no more than eighteen inches and it was virtually impossible for the slaves to turn or shift with any degree of ease. They lay during the six to ten weeks on the ocean voyage like living corpses. When epidemics of dysentery or smallpox swept through the ship, the dead bodies were thrown overboard. It was common for sharks to pick up a ship off the coast of Africa and follow it all the way to America.

CANDOR   The slave trade flourished in colonial America, and by the time of the American Revolution there were half a million black men living in enforced slavery in the colonies.

FIFTH READER *(remaining seated)*   Wasn't the slogan of that Revolution: "All men are created equal?" Why didn't it work out that way, if they had that idea in the beginning?

FIRST READER   Although the white colonists had won their political independence from England, they very nearly did not agree to form a union of states. A major cause of discord was the status of slaves. Northern spokesmen said that, since Southerners regarded slaves as mere property, they should not be included in the human count to determine representation in Congress. The question was not whether blacks should vote or not—obviously they should not vote—but should they be counted as human beings in the population statistics?

CANDOR   Why should the slaves of South Carolina be counted and not the horses of Massachusetts?

SECOND READER   Southern delegates demanded that Negroes be counted equally with whites so that the number of Southern congressmen would be as great as possible. However, Governor Morris of Pennsylvania said that his people would revolt if slaves were placed on an equal footing with white men. After heated debate, the delegates—white is the color of delegates—reached a compromise.

CANDOR   The compromise was written into the Constitution.

FIRST READER   Representatives shall be appointed among the States according to their population, which shall be determined by adding the number of free white persons, and three fifths of all black slaves, but excluding Indians.

CANDOR   Notice the color red appearing again. Not worth very much, but at least Indians got their name in the Constitution. White was worth one point. Black was worth three-fifths. Red was worth nothing.
     That was half of the compromise. The other half dealt with the institution of slave trade. Its opponents had hoped to put an end to it, but South Carolina said it would never accept a Constitution prohibiting the importation of slaves. So, they compromised, again.

SECOND READER   The importation of slaves shall not be prohibited by Congress prior to the year 1808.

CANDOR   In the years between the American Revolution and the Civil War, the demand for cotton fiber increased, and with it the de-

52

mand for black slaves. Since the Constitution prohibited the importation of slaves after 1807, slave breeding became an approved method of increasing the supply.

FIRST READER   Slave owners had certain male slaves solely for breeding. Planters gave inducements to the black women to have children, the most effective being a promise of freedom when the mother had a certain number of babies. Ten was the usual figure.

CANDOR   Blacks living under this system of human exploitation frequently revolted.

SECOND READER   As many as 250 slave uprisings and conspiracies occurred. All of them were virtually unsuccessful, because white was the color of power. To insure that this system functioned properly, each state had its slave code designed to keep slaves ignorant and in awe of white power. The police power of the states, the state militia and the U.S. Army stood behind these laws. In addition, the slave had to believe he was a slave, so slaves were taught that they were totally helpless and absolutely dependent upon their white masters.

CANDOR   Black became the color of absolute dependency. *(Pause)* By the time of the Civil War, we had four million black slaves in the United States. Among other things, the war was fought to change all that.

But the white power structure went to work on the post-Civil War apparatus so that freed blacks couldn't become free men.

FIRST READER   There is the story of the black man who appeared before a committee in the South to register as a voter. He had qualified at Harvard but the civil servant tried to catch him in every conceivable way, producing books in Latin and Greek, but all in vain. Finally, he pushed a Chinese newspaper under the nose of the black man and said: "Now, what does that mean?"

FIFTH READER *(remains seated, reads with animation)*   It means that you white folks are not going to let me vote.

CANDOR   That's right. White is the color of vote. Black is the color of no-vote. For the past hundred years, these systematic changes were so effective that they barred more than 95% of the blacks from voting, thereby virtually negating the purpose of the bloody sacrifices of the Civil War and nullifying the value of the Constitutional Amendments guaranteeing equal rights.

A man who is not color blind—who sees color very well—has been heard to ask, "What do they want?"

(FIFTH READER rises and walks onto the stage, saying in transit:)

FIFTH READER   I'll tell you what we want.

(FIFTH READER on stage, addresses the following words to CANDOR.)

FIFTH READER   We just don't want to belong. We just don't want to join. Okay? *(turns and addresses audience)* You've set up all the conditions, and then asked us in. No thanks. We don't want the things you want. We don't believe in your values. We couldn't live on your terms.

You say you want to help us. It ain't so, man. You just want to stay on top, and hand out the old welfare and last year's clothes, while we smile and shuffle kind of nice and say, "Thank you, sir." Well, we don't want you on top giving us anything.

You ask us to come in, but if we join your club we'll never be free. We'll never be our own boss. We won't be able to help ourselves.

So count us out. We're going to be playing in our own ball park, with our own rules.

(FIFTH READER returns to seat in audience.)

PART THREE

(CANDOR walks to easel. Removes black chart, places it face down on table. Returns to reading stand.)

CANDOR   The final color is brown. It's the color of almonds, and raw sugar. It's the color of the Philippines.

SECOND READER   By the time the United States got into the Spanish-American War, the Filipinos had been fighting a war of independence from Spain for more than six years.

FIRST READER   An independence movement, which began in 1892 with a few thousand laborers and peasants, had grown into a mass revolution with over 250,000 men. When the United States attacked the Spanish fleet at Manila Bay in 1898, the leader of the Filipino patriots and Admiral George Dewey were allies. But the revolutionary government feared that the United States might attempt to replace Spain as the colonial power over the Filipinos, so they proclaimed a Declaration of Independence in the name of the people of the Philippine Islands in June 1898.

SIXTH READER *(remaining seated)*   The declaration was ignored by the United States, wasn't it?

CANDOR   It seems so. The U.S. Army occupied the area around Manila. While the U.S. Congress debated the merits of granting the Filipinos their political independence and withdrawing our occupying army, hostilities broke out between American soldiers and Filipino nationals in 1899.

　　　When the Filipinos shifted to guerilla warfare, the U.S. Army Commander wired the War Department:

SECOND READER   With the kind of war we are up against now, to secure every town against attack would require more than the present complement of 5,000 combat troops.

SIXTH READER *(remaining seated)*   That all sure sounds familiar. *(Pause)* What were we doing there in the first place, in the Philippines seventy years ago?

CANDOR   President McKinley put it this way.

(THIRD READER rises and faces the audience.)

THIRD READER   The Spanish-American War has brought us new duties and responsibilities which we must meet and discharge as becomes a great nation on whose growth and career from the beginning the Ruler of all Nations has plainly written.

CANDOR   Senator Henry Cabot Lodge of Massachusetts, in 1900:

THIRD READER   China is the greatest market of them all. Our trade there is growing by leaps and bounds. Manila—the prize of war—gives us a tremendous advantage in developing that trade.

CANDOR   By 1902, U.S. investors were demanding that the U.S. clear away its restriction on granting franchises for business enterprises and mineral rights in the Philippine Islands.
William Howard Taft, U.S. Commissioner of the Philippines said:

THIRD READER   The seven million Filipinos are anxiously willing to follow American styles and American customs.

(THIRD READER sits down.)

SIXTH READER *(remaining seated)*   That's what we said. What were the Filipinos saying? What about their war for independence?

CANDOR   At the Paris Peace Conference, which was intended to settle the issues of the Spanish-American War, the Filipino delegation sought to present its credentials to the American Commission. They were denied a hearing. The Filipino said:

FIRST READER   We will not permit ourselves or our homes to be bought or sold like merchandise.

CANDOR   The Filipino leaders realized their political independence was in jeopardy, and they disbanded their regular army and shifted to guerilla warfare. But they were up against a formidable enemy. Virtually all of the ranking U.S. military commanders in the Philippines were veterans of the Indian Wars fought on the American Western Plains. The Secretary of War, in a speech, said:

SECOND READER   Utilizing the lessons of the Indian Wars, our army relentlessly follows the guerilla bands and crushes them.

CANDOR   Search and destroy. That was the tactic. Directives to troops under General J.H. Smith read:

FIRST READER   Every native, whether carrying arms or living in villages, will be regarded and treated as an enemy.

CANDOR   A survey of the conditions of certain regions six months later:

SECOND READER   The area had been a garden spot in the Philippines, covered with fine haciendas of sugar, coffee, tobacco and rice. Now it is desolate. Ninety percent of the water buffalos—the common work animals in the fields—have died or been slaughtered, rice crops reduced to one-fourth of normal production and a cholera epidemic is widespread. The area had to be destroyed in order to save it.

CANDOR   And there were massacres.

FIRST READER   In an American infantry assault in March 1906, over 600 Filipino men, women and children were killed. This massacre caused a wave of protest in the United States, especially when a photograph of the heaped bodies of women and children was printed in American newspapers.

CANDOR   And there were the prisons.

FIRST READER   During the pacification of the Filipinos fighting for their independence, the military jails were jammed with political prisoners. Conditions were appalling, prisoners suffering severe treatment, torture and starvation. As many as 300,000 Filipinos in one province were driven out of their homes and into detention camps.

CANDOR   Finally, with a volunteer army of 125,000 American troops, and fifteen years of fighting, and hundreds of thousands of Filipinos killed, the Philippine war of independence came to an end. The Philippine Islands became a Pacific outpost and, in 1946, the Philippines signed a treaty with the U.S. permitting America to use military facilities for ninety-nine years.

FIRST READER AND SECOND READER *(in unison)*   A-men.

CANDOR *(Pause)*   Well, that's it for the color test. Not all of the colors, of course. There is still a wide variety in the spectrum, like chicano brown, Devlin-Paisley green, ethnic white, yellow peril. But time's up. So, I guess that's it.

SIXTH READER   Wait a minute. We can't let it end there. *(Comes up onto the stage from back of the room. Addresses CANDOR)* All of these colors are the colors of discrimination and violence. Can't these colors mean anything else? I have a friend who sees other things in these colors—other possibilities. Let me read what he says. *(Takes a paper out of coat pocket and reads)*

57

Perhaps the day will come when our nation, distinguished by victories in past wars, and by the highest development of its military science, and accustomed to paying a high price for these things, will finally say *(Pause)* "We break our swords." We will dismantle our military machine. We, who have been the best armed, will then be unarmed. We will be armed with a real peace which rests on peace of mind, not the so-called armed peace as it now exists throughout the world. Nations trust neither themselves nor their neighbors. Half from hatred, half from fear, they do not lay down their weapons. Is it not better to perish rather than to hate and be afraid? And better to perish twice rather than force others to hate and fear us?

If we wish to be brothers, we must let the armaments fall from our hands. We cannot love others while we are holding weapons in our arms.

CANDOR   That's nonsense! *(Closes book, walks off stage and returns to seat in audience.)*

(SIXTH READER turns to FIRST READER who closes his book, walks off stage and returns to his seat in audience. SIXTH READER turns to SECOND READER who closes his book, walks off stage and returns to his seat in audience. SIXTH READER turns to audience.)

SIXTH READER   Is it? Is it nonsense? *(Music stops)*

END

Note: It is strongly recommended that sufficient time be allowed at the conclusion of the playlet for group discussion of the issues exhibited. The SIXTH READER should be prepared to lead the discussion.

First Things First

How well does the Federal Budget of the United States reflect our personal beliefs and priorities as U.S. citizens? Whose priorities does it reflect?

Background Reading:

From *A Call to Action* by Pope Paul VI

There is a need to establish a greater justice in the sharing of goods, both within national communities and on the international level. In international exchanges there is a need to go beyond relationships based on force, in order to arrive at agreements reached with the good of all in mind. Relationships based on force have never in fact established justice in a true and lasting manner, even if at certain times the alternation of positions can often make it possible to find easier conditions for dialogue. The use of force moreover leads to the setting in motion of opposing forces, and from this springs a climate of struggle which opens the way to situations of extreme violence and to abuses.

But, as we have often stated, the most important duty in the realm of justice is to allow each country to promote its own development, within the framework of a cooperation free from any spirit of domination, whether economic or political. The complexity of the problems raised is certainly great, in the present intertwining of mutual dependences. Thus it is necessary to have the courage to undertake a revision of the relationships between nations, whether it is a question of the international division of production, the structure of exchanges, the control of profits, the monetary system,—without forgetting the actions of human solidarity—to question the models of growth of the rich nations and change people's outlooks, so that they may realize the prior call of international duty, and to renew international organizations so that they may increase in effectiveness.

Under the driving force of new systems of production, national frontiers are breaking down, and we can see new economic powers emerging, the multinational enterprises, which by the concentration and flexibility of their means can conduct autonomous strategies which are largely independent of the national political powers and therefore not subject to control from the point of view of the common good. By extending their activities, these private organizations can lead to a new and abusive form of economic domination on the social, cultural and even political level. The excessive concentration of means and powers that Pope Pius XI already condemned on the fortieth anniversary of *Rerum Novarum* is taking on a new and very real image.

Change of attitudes and structures: Today men yearn to free themselves from need and dependence. But this liberation starts with the interior freedom that men must find again with regard to their goods and their powers; they will never reach it except through a transcendent love for man, and, in consequence, through a genuine readiness to serve. Otherwise, as one can see only too clearly, the most revolutionary ideologies lead only to a change of masters; once installed in power in their turn, these new masters surround themselves with privileges, limit freedoms and allow other forms of injustice to become established.

Thus many people are reaching the point of questioning the very model of society. The ambition of many nations, in the competition that sets them in opposition and which carries them along, is to attain technological, economic and military power. This ambition then stands in the way of setting up structures in which the rhythm of progress would be regulated with a view to greater justice, instead of accentuating inequalities and living in a climate of distrust and struggle which would unceasingly compromise peace.

Exercise

When you are asked to do so, place a mark in each of the 15 columns on the following chart to represent the amount of money that you estimate was allocated for each item in the 1972 Federal Budget of the United States. Remember that the total amount must come to no more than 176.8 billion dollars.

1972 Federal Budget: Total—176.8 billion dollars.

Billions of Dollars	National Defense	Veterans Benefits	Interest on War Debt	Education and Job Training	Health Care	Income Security	Agriculture and Rural Development	Natural Resources	Commerce and Transportation	Community Development and Housing	International Affairs	Space Research and Technology	General Government	Revenue Sharing	Other Expenditures
100															
95															
90															
85															
80															
75															
70															
65															
60															
55															
50															
45															
40															
35															
30															
25															
20															
15															
10															
5															
0															

MILITARY SPENDING			HUMAN RESOURCES			PHYSICAL RESOURCES				OTHERS				

The Global Village

What does the world look like when we shrink it down to a size that we can grasp?

Exercises

A. Imagine that the population of today's world could be reduced in proportion to one thousand people. Estimate how many people out of the thousand would live in each of these six areas:

North America _____	U.S.S.R. (Russia) _____
South America _____	Asia _____
Europe _____	Africa _____

B. If asked to do so, draw up a personal profile of the character you have been assigned to. Use the following questions as a guide:

What is your name? (choose a name native to the area)

Describe the general conditions of your life (health, education, and general welfare). How much personal security do you feel (for you and your family)?

If you are employed, what is your salary and how much job security do you have? If not employed, why not?

What is your estimated life expectancy? What are the chances that an infant child of yours will live to be two years old?

Why are you rich? OR Why are you poor?

If you could change one thing about your situation, what would it be?

The Coffee Game

Let's use just one product, coffee, to see if we can understand some of the workings of international political and economic systems.

Exercise

Read "Introduction to the Coffee Game" and "Introduction to Coffee in International Trade" on the following pages. When asked to do so, turn to the description of the role you will be assuming during the Coffee Game and read over the coversheet and the worksheet. Read only the coversheet and worksheet for the role to which you have been assigned.

Introduction to the Coffee Game

The Coffee Game covers a "two-year" period of time (mid-1971 to mid-1973) during which time (1) coffee and other products are exported from five Latin American countries; (2) wages to workers, income taxes, deposits in Swiss bank accounts, and fees for shipping and insurance services are paid; (3) imports are purchased from the United States; and (4) two conferences are held: the Conference of American States and the International Coffee Conference.

As a participant in the Coffee Game you will be asked by the Director to play one of these roles: a government representative or coffee grower from either Brazil, Colombia, Ecuador, El Salvador, or Guatemala; a banker, an import or export agent, or a foreign aid official from the United States; or, finally, a chairperson for one or both of the two conferences.

To aid you in playing the assigned role you will have a *coversheet* describing your position within your country, the role you will play in the Coffee Game and the schedule of the game. You will also have a *worksheet* that will guide you step-by-step through the game.

Since actual statistics on coffee trade are used in the Coffee Game you will merely be dramatizing and illustrating the realities of international trade and aid as you play your role. In this sense the winners and losers are already programmed into the game. Rather than try to "beat the game," you are encouraged to play faithful to the directions on your worksheet so that you will observe how—in reality—the winners use the "rules of the game" to their own advantage and to the disadvantage of the losers.

Introduction to Coffee in International Trade

Coffee is the single largest commodity in international trade, apart from petroleum. About twenty million people in forty-one coffee-producing countries depend on coffee for their livelihood. In Latin America alone, coffee is the breadwinner for about eleven million people. Hundreds of thousands of people are employed in the coffee industries of the five Latin American countries represented in the Coffee Game.

These five countries, Brazil, Colombia, Ecuador, El Salvador, and Guatemala, are basically "one-crop economies," that is, they depend on the sale of just one crop, coffee, for from 17 to 52 percent of the money they use every year to pay for goods and services imported from the United States.

With these export earnings Latin American countries can import machine tools from Cambridge, Massachusetts; foundry equipment from Dubuque, Iowa; aluminum products from Phoenix, Arizona; and many other U.S.-made goods and U.S.-grown farm products. At least 1,160 U.S. cities, towns, and communities in all of the 50 states benefit from the 339,000 jobs and the almost 3 billion dollars in wages and farm income that are stimulated by U.S. exports to Latin American coffee-producing countries.

The U.S. coffee industry imports bags of unroasted coffee from Latin America. This unroasted coffee is then processed, packaged, distributed and sold by the U.S. coffee industry. U.S. control of the processing of coffee generates about 175,000 jobs for U.S. workers and about one billion dollars in wages.

You represent the COFFEE GROWERS' ORGANIZATION OF A LATIN AMERICAN COUNTRY

YOUR POSITION WITHIN YOUR COUNTRY

Your position as the representative of the Coffee Growers' Organization puts you in the top one-fifth of the population which absorbs about 60 per cent of the total national income. By contrast the lowest one-fifth of the population receives only 3 per cent of the income. You and the other members of your class (including the Representative of your government) have the power to determine the direction of your country's development and its industrialization. You choose which products will be imported from abroad and you decide how resources will be allocated throughout the country. Though the pressures of your position may be great you are assured of a personal life of luxury and of a future guaranteed by the fortunes in your Swiss bank account.

YOUR ROLE IN THE COFFEE GAME

As the representative of the Coffee Growers' Organization you will be primarily responsible for the annual sale of your country's coffee crop, for the payment of income taxes, and for the care of the workers on all levels of the coffee industry. You will be invited to participate as an observer at the Conference of American States (CAS) and you will be a certified delegate at the International Coffee Conference (ICC).

Your dealings thoughout the game will be principally with three people: the U.S. Import Agent, the Branch Officer of the U.S. Bank, and the Representative of your country's government. Note who these players are when the game begins.

THE GAME SCHEDULE

When the Director signals the start of the Coffee Game you should begin working through the steps outlined on your worksheet.

1 SELL EXPORTS

Your first task in the Coffee Game will be to bring your coffee crop to the
U.S. Import Agent for sale. The Agent determines how much of your
coffee he will take and how much you will be paid. In a typical year
Brazil exports about $370 million worth of coffee to the United States. At
the start of the game the Import Agent will pay the Brazilian Representative in chips equivalent to $3.70 for the 1971 coffee crop.

Export Earnings for Other Countries:

	COFFEE EXPORTS TO THE U.S.	1971 EXPORT EARNINGS
COLOMBIA	$160 million	$1.60
ECUADOR	$ 20 million	.20
EL SALVADOR	$ 30 million	.30
GUATEMALA	$ 30 million	.30

2 PAY TAXES

Upon receipt of these "export earnings" you must pay the Income Taxes of the Coffee Growers' Organization to the representative of your government. The representative will estimate how much Income Tax you owe the government (usually about 20% of your "export earnings" from the sale of coffee). The government uses these taxes to purchase the imports it purchases from abroad each year and to cover expenses for transportation services rendered by U.S. shippers and banks.

3 SWISS BANK ACCOUNTS

Before paying out any more money you will want to provide for your own personal security and that of your fellow coffee growers. So, from the cash you have on hand, you will make a deposit into the Branch Office of the U.S. Bank for your personal Swiss bank account.

BRAZIL — an annual deposit of 75 cents;
COLOMBIA — 25 cents annually;
ECUADOR, EL SALVADOR, GUATEMALA — 10 cents each annually.

This sum of money is untouchable until the end of the game (that is, until you "leave the country"). It should not be considered "cash on hand," nor should it be figured in under the heading "money paid out," in the Year-End Financial Statement you will prepare for the Coffee Conference.

4 PAY WORKERS

Having provided for your own needs your next responsibility is to the workers in the coffee industry. It is up to you to decide how much money should be put aside in the Branch Office of the U.S. Bank each year for their salaries. To forestall the possibility of all-out revolution, however, you must pay them at least the minimum salary indicated on the scale below. Pay them either from cash on hand or from loans taken from the Branch Office of the U.S. Bank.

If at any time during the game you need extra money over and above that which you receive for the sale of your coffee crop, contact the Branch Office of the U.S. Bank to arrange for a loan.

Scale of Workers' Salaries

BRAZIL: If you wish each one of the six million workers in your coffee industry to receive an annual salary of $50, then give the Branch Office of the U.S. Bank chips equivalent to $3 in cash. This lump sum of money would be divided up among all the workers by the U.S. Banker. Every additional $3 that you give to the Banker represents an additional $50 a year that each worker would be receiving. Thus, $6 represents a salary of $100 a year; $9 equals $150 a year; and $12 equals $200 a year.

COLOMBIA: If you wish each one of the two million workers in your coffee industry to receive an annual salary of $50, then give the Branch Office of the U.S. Bank chips equivalent to $1 in cash. This lump sum of money would be divided up among all the workers by the U.S. Banker. Every additional $1 that you give to the Banker represents an additional $50 a year that each worker would be receiving. Thus, $2 represents a salary of $100 a year; $3 equals $150 a year; $4 equals $200 a year; and $5 equals $250 a year.

ECUADOR, EL SALVADOR, GUATEMALA: If you wish each one of the 400,000 workers in your coffee industry to receive an annual salary of $50, then give the Branch Office of the U.S. Bank chips equivalent to 25 cents in cash. This lump sum of money would be divided up among all the workers by the U.S. Banker. Every additional 25 cents that you give to the Banker represents an additional $50 a year that each worker would be receiving. Thus, 50 cents represents a salary of $100 a year; 75 cents equals $150 a year; $1 equals $200 a year; and $1.25 equals $250 a year.

5 YEAR-END FINANCIAL STATEMENT

Keep a record of your financial transactions on the worksheet so that you will be prepared to deliver a Year-End Financial Statement at the International Coffee Conferences in 1972 and 1973.

1971 WORKSHEET for the Representatives of the Coffee Growers' Organization

1. Sell your coffee crop to the U.S. Import Agent.

    Received: _____

2. Pay Income Taxes to your Government Representative.

    Paid: _____

3. Make a deposit into your personal Swiss bank account.

    Paid: _____

4. Pay the workers in your country's coffee industry.

    Paid: _____

    (You must pay them at least the minimum salary indicated on your coversheet.)

    Record the total amount of money you have on hand: _____

5. Prepare a Year-End Financial Statement using the questions below.

    Attend the 1972 Conference of American States as an observer.

    Attend the 1972 International Coffee Conference and deliver your Financial Statement when called upon to do so by the Chairperson.

1971 Year-End Financial Statement of the Coffee Growers' Organization (for presentation at the 1972 ICC)

A. How much money did you take in this year from the sale of your coffee?

B. How much money did you pay out this year in taxes and workers' salaries? (Do *not* figure in deposits in your Swiss bank account).

C. How much money do you owe the Branch Office of the U.S. Bank? How much money do you have in your Swiss bank account?

D. Do you have any general comment to make about your relationships with either your workers, your government, or the U.S. agents?

1972 WORKSHEET for the Representatives of the Coffee Growers' Organization

1. Sell your coffee crop to the U.S. Import Agent.

    Received: _____

2. Pay Income Taxes to your Government Representative.

    Paid: _____

3. Make a deposit into your personal Swiss bank account.

    Paid: _____

4. Pay the workers in your country's coffee industry.

    Paid: _____

    Record the total amount of money you have on hand: _____

5. Prepare a Year-End Financial Statement using the questions below.

    Attend the 1973 Conference of American States as an observer.

    Attend the 1973 International Coffee Conference and deliver your Financial Statement when called upon to do so by the Chairperson.

1972 Year-End Financial Statement of the Coffee Growers' Organization (for presentation at the 1973 ICC)

A. How much money did you take in this year from the sale of your coffee?

B. How much money did you pay out this year in taxes and workers' salaries? (Do *not* figure in deposits in your Swiss bank account).

C. How much money do you owe the Branch Office of the U.S. Bank?

    How much money do you have in your Swiss bank account?

D. Do you have any general comment to make about your relationships with either your workers, your government, or the U.S. agents?

You represent a LATIN AMERICAN GOVERNMENT

YOUR ROLE IN THE COFFEE GAME

As a representative of the government you will be primarily responsible for the annual sale of your country's exports of products *other than coffee* and for the purchase of imports from the United States. These transactions will be carried out with the U.S. Import Agent and the U.S. Export Agent respectively. The Representative of the Coffee Growers' Organization will handle the annual sale of your country's coffee crop.

It will also be your responsibility to collect income taxes and to pay the transportation charges for shipping and banking services rendered by U.S. firms. You will attend the annual International Coffee Conferences (ICC) as an observer and you will be a certified delegate to the Conferences of American States (CAS) at the start of years 1972 and 1973.

Your dealings thoughout the game will be principally with four people: the U.S. Import Agent, the U.S. Export Agent, the Representative of the Main Office of the U.S. Bank, and the Representative of your country's Coffee Growers' Organization. Note who these players are when the game begins.

YOUR POSITION WITHIN YOUR COUNTRY

Your position as Representative of the Government puts you in the top one-fifth of the population which absorbs about 60% of the total national income. By contrast the lowest one-fifth of the population receives only 3% of the income. You and the other members of your class (including the Coffee Growers) have the power to determine the direction of your country's development and its industrialization. You choose which products will be imported from abroad and you decide how resources will be allocated throughout the country. Though the pressures of your position may be great, you are assured of a personal life of luxury and of a future guaranteed by the fortunes in your Swiss bank account.

THE GAME SCHEDULE

When the Director signals the start of the Coffee Game you should begin working through the steps outlined on your worksheet.

1 SELL EXPORTS

Your first task in the Coffee Game will be to bring your country's exports to the U.S. Import Agent for sale. The Agent determines the volume and the price of the exports he will purchase from you. In a typical year Brazil's exports to the United States total about $670 million. Of this total $300 million worth are for exports *other than* coffee. At the start of the game the U.S. Import Agent will pay the Brazilian Representative in chips equivalent to $3.00 for 1971 exports.

Export Earnings for Other Countries:

	TOTAL EXPORTS TO THE U.S.	EXPORTS OTHER THAN COFFEE	1971 EXPORT EARNINGS
COLOMBIA	$265 million	$100 million	$1.00
ECUADOR	$ 90 million	$ 70 million	.70
EL SALVADOR	$ 45 million	$ 20 million	.20
GUATEMALA	$ 70 million	$ 35 million	.35

2 COLLECT TAXES

You will need extra revenue to cover the costs of imports from the United States and so your next responsibility in the game will be the collection of Income Taxes from the Coffee Growers' Organization. You can assess them as much as you want. Twenty-five per cent of their earnings from the sale of coffee (rounded out to the nickel) is the normal rate. If a coffee grower refuses to pay any Income Taxes you can ask the U.S. Bank to withhold any further loans to that Organization.

3 PAY SERVICE CHARGES

Since most of the exports from your country are transported in U.S. ships and insured by U.S. banks, you will have to pay the U.S. Import Agent service charges according to the following scale:

BRAZIL — an annual service charge of 50 cents;
COLOMBIA — 25 cents annually;
ECUADOR, EL SALVADOR, GUATEMALA — 10 cents each annually.

4 SWISS BANK ACCOUNTS

Before paying out any other money you will want to provide for your own personal security and that of your fellow government officials. So, from the cash you have on hand, you will make a deposit into the Main Office of the U.S. Bank for your personal Swiss bank account:

BRAZIL — an annual deposit of 75 cents;
COLOMBIA — 25 cents annually;
ECUADOR, EL SALVADOR, GUATEMALA — 10 cents annually.

This sum of money is untouchable until the end of the game (that is, until you "leave the country"). It should not be considered "cash on hand," nor should it be figured in under the heading "money paid out," in the Year-End Financial Statement you will prepare for the Coffee Conference of American States.

5 BUY IMPORTS

Next you will have to prepare for the purchase of imports from the United States to meet your country's needs in the coming year. This transaction will be carried out immediately after the 1972 and 1973 International Coffee Conferences. Before the Conference of American States you should consult with the U.S. Export Agent to see how much you will have to pay for imports from the United States. Then, see the Main Office of the U.S. Bank and arrange for any loans you may need to meet projected costs.

6 YEAR-END FINANCIAL STATEMENT

Keep a record of your financial transactions on the worksheet so that you will be prepared to deliver a Year-End Financial Statement at the 1972 and 1973 Conferences of American States.

1971 WORKSHEET for the
Government Representatives

1. Sell your exports to the U.S. Import Agent.

    Received: _____

2. Collect Income Taxes from the Coffee Growers.

    Received: _____

3. Pay the U.S. Import Agent for transportation services.

    Paid: _____

4. Make a deposit into your personal Swiss bank account.

    Paid: _____

    Record the total amount of money you have on hand: _____

5. Consult with the U.S. Export Agent to see how much you will have to pay for goods imported from the U.S. in 1972. Do *not* pay for these imports until after the 1972 International Coffee Conference.

    Arrange for needed loans from the U.S. Bank so that you will be able to meet projected expenditures for imports from the U.S.

6. Prepare a Year-End Financial Statement using questions below.

    Attend the 1972 Conference of American States and deliver your Financial Statement when called upon to do so by the Chairperson.

    Attend the 1972 International Coffee Conference as an observer.

1971 Year-End Financial Statement
of the Governmental Representatives
(for presentation at the 1972 CAS)

A. How much money did you take in this year in payment for your exports and income taxes?

B. How much money did you have to pay out this year? (Do *not* figure in the money you have in your Swiss bank account.)

C. How much money do you owe the Main Office of the U.S. Bank? How much money do you have in your Swiss bank account?

D. Do you have any general comment to make on the state of your country or on its relationship to the United States?

1972 WORKSHEET for the
Government Representatives

Buy the imports you need from the U.S. Export Agent *after* the 1972 International Coffee Conference.

Paid: _____

1. Sell your exports to the U.S. Import Agent.

    Received: _____

2. Collect Income Taxes from the Coffee Growers.

    Received: _____

3. Pay the U.S. Import Agent for transportation services.

    Paid: _____

4. Make a deposit into your personal Swiss bank account.

    Paid: _____

    Record the total amount of money you have on hand:_____

5. Consult with the U.S. Export Agent to see how much you will have to pay for goods imported from the United States in 1973. (Again, do *not* pay for these imports now. You will do so after the 1973 ICC.)

    Arrange for needed loans from the U.S. Bank so that you will be able to meet projected expenditures for imports from the United States.

6. Prepare a Year-End Financial Statement using the questions below.

    Attend the 1973 Conference of American States and deliver your Financial Statement when called upon to do so by the Chairperson.

    Attend the 1973 International Coffee Conference as an observer.

1972 Year-End Financial Statement
of the Governmental Representatives
(for presentation at the 1973 CAS)

A. How much money did you take in this year in payment for your exports and income taxes?

B. How much money did you have to pay out this year for imports from the U.S. and for other expenses? (Excluding deposits in your Swiss bank account.)

C. How much money do you owe the Main Office of the U.S. Bank? How much money has accumulated in your personal Swiss bank account?

D. Do you have any general comment to make on the state of your country or on its relationship to the United States?

You are the U.S. IMPORT AGENT

YOUR ROLE IN THE COFFEE GAME

As the U.S. Import Agent you will be primarily responsible for the purchase of all exports coming each year from the Latin American countries of Brazil, Colombia, Ecuador, El Salvador, and Guatemala. These exports include: (1) *coffee* from the Representatives of the Coffee Growers' Organization, and (2) *other products* from the Representatives of the various Latin American governments. During the course of the Coffee Game your dealings will be principally with the Representative of the Main Office of the U.S. Bank and with the Representatives from the five Latin American countries. Note who these players are when the game begins.

THE GAME SCHEDULE

When the Director signals the start of the Coffee Game you should begin working through the steps outlined on your worksheet.

When the Coffee Game begins the representatives of Latin American countries and Coffee Growers' Organizations will come to you to receive payment for their exports. You can help to eliminate a bottleneck at the very start of the Coffee Game by following these steps immediately:

(1) See the Representative of the Main Office of the U.S. Bank to receive enough chips to cover the amounts that you will have to pay out for Latin America's 1971 exports.

You will need about 30 white chips, 15 red, and 15 blue chips to begin the game. Money is always available to you *without interest* from the U.S. Banks.

(2) Ask the Representative of the Main Office of the U.S. Bank to help you prepare and distribute the chips to the Representatives of the Latin American governments and Coffee Growers' Organizations according to the following scale for 1971:

1971	GOVERNMENT	COFFEE GROWERS' ORGANIZATION
BRAZIL	$3.00	$3.70
COLOMBIA	1.00	1.60
ECUADOR	.70	.20
EL SALVADOR	.20	.30
GUATEMALA	.35	.35

After you have paid the Representatives from Latin America for their exports each year you will receive from the Representatives of the governments payment for the transportation services rendered by U.S. shippers and banks. If any government falls behind in payment for these services notify the Officer at the Main Office of the U.S. Bank to withhold any future loans.

You will attend the Conference of American States (CAS) and the International Coffee Conference (ICC) at the start of years 1972 and 1973 in the game. At the ICC you will be called upon to announce the prices to be paid for the exports you will purchase from Latin America in that coming year. You may also be called upon to explain any rise or fall in prices and volume of exports (see your worksheets for 1972 and 1973).

1971 WORKSHEET for the
U.S. Import Agent

1. Pay for the exports of the Latin American governments and Coffee Growers' Organization according to the scale on your coversheet.

2. Receive payment from the Latin American governments for U.S. transportation services according to the following scale:

   BRAZIL — 50 cents;
   COLOMBIA — 25 cents;
   ECUADOR, EL SALVADOR, GUATEMALA — 10 cents each.

3. Prepare the money you will need in 1972. Consult the 1972 scale below. (Cf. 1972 Worksheet, numbers 1 and 3).

4. Attend the 1972 Conference of American States and the International Coffee Conference.

1972 WORKSHEET

1. At the *1972 International Coffee Conference* announce the terms of the 1972 Coffee Agreement when called upon to do so by the Chairperson of the meeting. They are as follows:

— "*BRAZIL*, there have been rumors that you are considering the processing of your own coffee crop. You know as well as we do that such action on your part would hurt the U.S. job market. We wish to register our displeasure by purchasing only *$3.50* worth of your coffee this year."

— "*COLOMBIA*, the political unrest and rumors of communist subversion in your country have made coffee interests here in the United States a bit apprehensive. We think it safe to purchase only *$1.50* worth of your coffee this year."

— "*ECUADOR*, the displeasure of the U.S. Government over the seizure of some U.S. tunaboats makes coffee interests hesitant to do much business with you this year. We will take only *15 cents worth of your coffee exports.*"

– "*EL SALVADOR*, we have taken note of the losses you suffered last year due to the sudden frost. We will increase the volume of coffee we import from El Salvador this year bringing the total to *50 cents.*"

— "*GUATEMALA*, the rising costs of processing coffee in the United States make it impossible for the U.S. coffee industry to take any more coffee from you than we did last year. So, we will take 35 *cents* worth of your coffee exports."

2. Immediately after the 1972 International Coffee Conference distribute the money you owe to the various Coffee Growers' Organizations according to the terms of the above 1972 Coffee Agreement.

3. *NOTE:* You will also be purchasing exports from the Latin American governments (in addition to the Coffee Growers). So, in 1972 you will pay out:

	COFFEE GROWERS	GOVERNMENTS
BRAZIL	$3.50	$3.25
COLOMBIA	1.50	.90
ECUADOR	.15	.50
EL SALVADOR	.50	.25
GUATEMALA	.35	.40

4. Receive payment from the Latin American governments for U.S. transportation services according to the 1971 scale (Cf. 1971 Worksheet, number 2).

5. The Coffee Game ends after the 1973 ICC, so there is no need to prepare money for payment in that year.

6. Attend the 1973 CAS and ICC.

1973 WORKSHEET

At the *1973 ICC* announce the following terms of the 1973 Agreement:

— "*BRAZIL*, we are sorry to see that you have gone through with your threats to begin the processing of your own coffee. While this may have some short-range benefits for your economy we hope that you fully understand the effects such moves are having on the U.S. economy. The U.S. Coffee Industry has U.S. jobs to protect and we will not be undersold. Our purchase of only *$3* worth of your coffee exports this year should be a sign to you of the depth of our displeasure."

—"*COLOMBIA*, the speed with which your government acted to put down the unrest among the peasants and workers in your country is a very encouraging sign. We will be purchasing $1.80 worth of your coffee this year."

—"ECUADOR, we are happy to see that your government has been exercising great restraint with regard to U.S. fishing rights in your area. Though we would like to be able to take more of your coffee crop this year we are sorry to report that there has been a slight drop on the U.S. market in the demand for coffee and so we will be able to purchase only 20 cents worth."

—"EL SALVADOR, we realize that you are still suffering the effects of last year's frost. We wish we could be of more help to you, but the extremely good prices available from the coffee markets in Africa are too good a deal to pass up. We will take only 40 cents worth of your coffee this year."

—"GUATEMALA, we are unable to take any more of your coffe exports than we took last year. Once again we will take 35 cents worth."

NOTE: The Coffee Game ends after the 1973 ICC so there is no need to prepare payments for any Latin American exports.

You are the U.S. EXPORT AGENT

YOUR ROLE IN THE COFFEE GAME

As the U.S. Export Agent you will be primarily responsible for the sale of all U.S. exports to the countries of Brazil, Colombia, Ecuador, El Salvador, and Guatemala. Your dealings throughout the game will be with the U.S. Bankers and with the Representatives of the Latin American governments. Note who these players are when the game begins.

THE GAME SCHEDULE

When the Director signals the start of the Coffee Game the Latin American countries will sell their exports (coffee and other products) to the U.S. Import Agent. With the money they receive, the Representatives of the Coffee Growers' Organizations have to pay their Income Taxes and workers' salaries, and the Representatives of the governments have to pay the costs of transportation services rendered by U.S. banks and shipping firms.

At the start of years 1972 and 1973 in the Coffee Game two conferences will be held: the Conference of American States and the International Coffee Conference. You will attend the Conferences of American States when they are convened.

At the Conference of American States you will be called upon to announce to the Latin American countries the amount of money that each country owes for the imports it is purchasing from the United States. The Representatives of each of the governments will have seen you prior to the CAS, so they will already know how much they owe and they will be prepared to pay you for the imports immediately *after* the International Coffee Conferences. Your purpose in announcing the prices of U.S. exports at the CAS is to make everyone aware of the reasons why prices increase from year to year. The reasons are included on your worksheet.

WORKSHEET for the
U.S. Export Agent

1971:   At the *1972 Conference of American States* the Chairperson will ask you to announce the sums of money that each Latin American government will have to pay for the U.S. exports it requested. In 1972, they are as follows:

"The *Government of Brazil* owes $7 for machinery, chemicals, wheat, copper, aircraft and parts."

"The *Goverment of Colombia* owes $3 for machinery, chemicals, wheat, primary metals, and motor vehicles and parts."

"The *Government of El Salvador* owes 60 *cents* for machinery, chemicals, wheat, paper, and motor vehicles and parts."

"The *Government of Ecuador* owes $1 for machinery, paper, chemicals and products, and motor vehicles and parts."

"The *Government of Guatemala* owes 90 *cents* for machinery, chemicals, textile fabrics, paper, and motor vehicles and parts."

You should explain to those in attendance at the Conference that the overall costs for U.S. exports are rising because of increasing union demands in the United States for higher wages and benefits for their workers.

Collect the above sums of money from the governments represented at the Conference immediately after the International Coffee Conference in 1972.

If a government does not have enough money on hand to pay for the imports it needs, then it must borrow the amount needed from the Main Office of the U.S. Bank. If you do not receive payment for the exports you are selling to a particular country, instruct the U.S. Import Agent not to accept any imports from that country for 1972.

1972:   At the *1973 Conference of American States* the Chairperson will ask you to announce the sums of money that each Government Representative will have to pay for the U.S. exports it requested. For 1973, they are as follows:

"The *Government of Brazil* owes $8 for its import needs. The rise over last year's costs is due to the larger amounts of wheat that we are sending you for your ever-growing population."

"The *Government of Colombia* owes $3.50 for its import needs. Though we are sending you only as much machinery as we did last year we are certain that you understand that the increased costs are due to the rising cost of living in the United States."

"The *Government of El Salvador* owes *65 cents* for its import needs."

"The *Government of Guatemala* owes *$1.10* and the *Government of Ecuador* owes the same amount for the imports that each will need in 1973. The increased costs this year are due to the fact that you are now importing parts and services for the machinery we sold you last year."

The Coffee Game ends after the 1973 International Coffee Conference, so there will be no need to collect this money from the Government Representatives.

You are the
CHAIRPERSON of the UNITED STATES BANK

YOUR ROLE IN THE COFFEE GAME

As Chairperson of the Main Office of the U.S. Bank it will be your responsibility to keep all U.S. agents supplied with cash and to handle all requests for loans from the Representatives of the Latin American *governments.* You will also oversee and direct the operations of the Branch Offices of the U.S. Bank which deal directly with the Representatives of the Coffee Growers' Organizations of each country.

Your dealings throughout the Coffee Game will be primarily with nine people: The U.S. Import Agent, the U.S. Foreign Aid Official, the two Branch Officers of the U.S. Bank, and the Government Representatives from the five Latin American countries. Note who these players are when the game begins.

YOUR POSITION IN THE UNITED STATES

Your position as the Chairperson of the U.S. Bank places you in the top one per cent of the U.S. population which holds between 20 and 30 per cent of all personal wealth in the United States. You and the other members of your class hold 72 per cent of all corporate stock in the United States. Your personal wealth puts you in the class of a "millionaire." It is quite possible that you were one of the 21 millionaires who evaded the payment of any federal taxes at all in 1967.

Your personal wealth gives you enormous political power, too. It is possible that you were one of the 12 bankers who served on the prestigious and powerful House Banking Commission during the 90th Congress. Such a position enables you to guarantee legislation that will be of benefit to you personally and to the other members of your class.

THE GAME SCHEDULE

When the Director signals the start of the Coffee Game you should begin working through the steps outlined on your worksheet.

At the start of the game the Latin American exporters will sell their 1971 exports of coffee and other products to the U.S. Import Agent. Following that, Income Taxes and fees for transportation services are paid, deposits are made in Swiss bank accounts, and workers in the Latin America coffee industry are paid. At the start of each year in the Coffee Game, two conferences are held: the Conference of American States (CAS) with Representatives of each of the Latin American governments and the International Coffee Conference (ICC) with Representatives of the Coffee Growers' Organizations of each country. At the CAS the Latin American governments arrange for the purchase of U.S. exports from the U.S. Export Agent and make their requests for U.S. foreign aid.

Even before the Director signals the start of the game the U.S. Import Agent will be coming to you to obtain enough money to cover the purchases of Latin America's exports for 1971. The Agent will also ask you to help distribute this money to the Latin American exporters in this first round of the Coffee Game. This will help avoid a bottleneck at the start of the game.

Throughout the game you should make all the money in the Main Office of the U.S. Bank available without interest to all the Branch Offices and to all U.S. agents.

You will handle all loans requested by the Representatives of the Latin American governments. (Refer loan requests by Coffee Growers to the Branch Offices of your bank.) They can borrow as much money as they want—provided their credit is good with the other U.S. agents. Add 10 per cent interest to each loan you dispense and advise the Government Representative that you are doing so. NOTE: *No* bank loans (including interest) will be re-paid before the end of the Coffee Game, so there is no need to keep very detailed records of loans accumulating interest. Simply make sure that the Government Representative understands that interest is mounting up on the outstanding debt.

The Government Representatives will be making deposits into their special Swiss bank accounts through your office. You will receive this money in the following amounts: from Brazil, 75 cents; from Colombia, 25 cents; and from Ecuador, El Salvador, and Guatemala, 10 cents. Keep a record of these deposits on your worksheet.

Attend both the Conference of American States and the International Coffee Conference at the start of years 1972 and 1973 in the game.

You are the
BRANCH OFFICER OF THE UNITED STATES BANK

YOUR ROLE IN THE COFFEE GAME

As the Branch Officer of the U.S. Bank it will be your responsibility to handle all financial dealings with the Representatives of the Coffee Growers' Organizations from Latin America. (The Chairman of the Main Office of the U.S. Bank will deal directly with the Government Representatives from Latin America.) You will make loans to the Coffee Growers' Organizations and receive from them the wages that they set aside for the workers each year. Your dealings throughout the Coffee Game will be primarily with six people: the Chairman of the Main Office of the U.S. Bank and the Representatives of the five Latin American Coffee Growers' Organizations. Note who these players are when the Coffee Game begins.

YOUR POSITION IN THE UNITED STATES

Your position as the Branch Officer of the U.S. Bank places you in the top fifth of the U.S. population with regard to wealth and income. You and the

other members of your class receive more *income* each year than the bottom
60 per cent of American families. The top fifth receives close to half of all
wages and salaries; 65 per cent of all unearned or property income; and
holds 97 per cent of all corporate stock. As far as personal *wealth* is concerned, your class owns over three-quarters of all personal wealth in the
United States. Your personal income exceeds $200 thousand a year, and it is
likely that you are one of the 155 such income earners who paid no federal
taxes at all in 1968.

Your personal wealth gives you enormous political power, too. It is
possible that you were one of the 27 bankers in the House of Representatives
during the 90th Congress. Such a prestigious position enables you to
guarantee legislation that will be of benefit to you personally and to the other
members of your class.

THE GAME SCHEDULE

When the Director signals the start of the Coffee Game you should begin
working through the steps outlined on your worksheet. Throughout the
Coffee Game you will be free to transfer any sums of money you need from
the Main Office of the U.S. Bank to your Branch Office. This same money is
always available to U.S. agents without interest.

At the very start of the game the Latin American exporters will sell their
1971 exports to the U.S. Import Agent. Following that, Income Taxes and
fees for transportation services are paid, deposits are made in Swiss bank
accounts, and workers in the Latin American coffee industry must be paid.

You will make all loans to the Coffee Growers' Organization. They can
borrow as much money as they want—provided their credit is good with the
other U.S. agents. Add 10 per cent interest to each loan you dispense and
advise the Coffee Grower that you are doing so. *NOTE: No* bank loans

(including interest) will be repaid before the end of the Coffee Game, so there is no need to keep very detailed records of loans and accumulating interest. Simply make sure that the Coffee Grower understands that interest is mounting up on the outstanding debt.

The Coffee Growers will be making deposits into their special Swiss bank accounts through your office. You will receive this money in the following amounts: from Brazil, 75 cents; from Colombia, 25 cents; and from Ecuador, El Salvador, and Guatemala, 10 cents. Keep a record of these deposits on your worksheet.

Workers' Salaries

The wages given to you by the Coffee Growers' Organizations will vary according to the number of workers employed by the coffee industry in each Latin American country and according to how much the representative is able to pay each year. The Coffee Growers will compute the salaries themselves according to the following sliding scale:

BRAZIL   each $3 worth of chips that the representative gives to you represents a yearly salary of $50 that each one of the workers in the Brazilian coffee industry would receive;

COLOMBIA   each $1 worth of chips that the representative gives to you represents a yearly salary of $50 that each one of the workers in the Colombian coffee industry would receive;

ECUADOR, EL SALVADOR, AND GUATEMALA   each 25 cents that the representative of each of these countries gives to you represents a yearly salary of $50 that each one of the workers in the respective coffee industries would receive.

Banker's WORKSHEET

1. Keep records of loans made to the representatives of the Latin American governments and coffee growers.

RECORD OF LOANS:	Loan	+	10% Interest	=	Total	
BRAZIL	_____	+	_____	=	_____	1971
	_____	+	_____	=	_____	1972
					_____	1973
COLOMBIA	_____	+	_____	=	_____	1971
	_____	+	_____	=	_____	1972
					_____	1973
ECUADOR	_____	+	_____	=	_____	1971
	_____	+	_____	=	_____	1972
					_____	1973
EL SALVADOR	_____	+	_____	=	_____	1971
	_____	+	_____	=	_____	1972
					_____	1973
GUATEMALA	_____	+	_____	=	_____	1971
	_____	+	_____	=	_____	1972
					_____	1973

2. Collect and record deposits in the Swiss bank accounts.

	1971	+	1972	=	1973 Total
BRAZIL – yearly deposit of 75 cents:	____	+	____	=	_____
COLOMBIA – yearly deposit of 25 cents:	____	+	____	=	_____
ECUADOR – yearly deposit of 10 cents:	____	+	____	=	_____
EL SALVADOR – yearly deposit of 10 cents:	____	+	____	=	_____
GUATEMALA – yearly deposit of 10 cents:	____	+	____	=	_____

NOTE to Chairperson of the U.S. Bank

— see to it that all U.S. Agents have free access to the money in your bank;

— assist the U.S. Import Agent in preparing and paying for the *1971* exports of coffee and other products from Latin America.

NOTE to Branch Officers of the U.S. Bank

—keep a record of the workers' salaries paid to you by the Latin American coffee growers;

Record of WORKERS' SALARIES RECEIVED:	1971	1972
BRAZIL	_____	_____
COLOMBIA	_____	_____
ECUADOR	_____	_____
EL SALVADOR	_____	_____
GUATEMALA	_____	_____

94

You are the
U.S. FOREIGN AID OFFICIAL

YOUR ROLE IN THE COFFEE GAME

At the 1972 Conference of American States the Chairperson of the CAS will ask you to announce the sums of U.S. foreign aid that are available to those governments who request them. You should emphasize in your statement at the CAS that these sums of foreign aid are *loans* that must be repaid with an accumulating interest of 5 per cent compounded annually. Foreign aid loans are available just to governments and only under the conditions stipulated below.

"In 1972 the United States will make the following sums of money available to the Representatives of Latin American governments in foreign aid:

— "To the *Government of Brazil* we offer $1 in foreign aid. We should warn you, though, that we would be very displeased to see the Brazilian Coffee Growers go through with their plans to begin processing their own coffee. We hope that you will use portions of this foreign aid loan to assist the coffee growers financially so that they will not have to resort to what would clearly be an attack on the jobs of U.S. processors of coffee;

— "To the *Government of Colombia* we offer 75 *cents* in foreign aid. There are still rumors of peasant unrest in Colombia and so we insist that if you accept this loan you must use 50 cents of it to purchase military hardware from the United States (*NOTE* to the Foreign Aid Official: If they accept the loan, you keep the 50 cents for military hardware, and give the Government Representative only 25 cents. Point out, also, that interest will be accumulating on the entire loan of 75 cents);

— "To the *Government of El Salvador* we offer 50 *cents* in foreign aid. Forty cents of this loan, however, will come to you in the form of 'Food for Peace.' The remainder will be a cash loan in emergency relief for those whose coffee crops were hard hit by the sudden frost last year. We trust that you will pass this relief money on to the poor coffee workers in El Salvador (*NOTE* to the Aid Official: If they accept this loan, you keep 40 cents to pay U.S. farmers for the food and give the Government Representative only 10 cents. Point out that interest will be accumulating on the entire loan of 50 cents);

— "To the *Government of Guatemala* we offer 75 *cents* in foreign aid. Fifty-five cents of this loan will be in the form of tractors and other farm machinery and the remainder will be a cash loan for you to use as you see fit (*NOTE* to the Aid Official: If they accept this loan, you keep 55

cents to pay for the manufacture and shipping of the tractors and give the Government Representative only 20 cents. Point out that interest will be accumulating on the entire loan of 75 cents);

— "To the *Government of Ecuador* we offer *35 cents* in foreign aid. We warn you, though, that we are extremely unhappy over your harassment of U.S. tunaboats. Continued harassment could result in the complete cutoff of all foreign aid."

Keep a record of how much each government takes from you in foreign aid. They will *not* be repaying you during the course of the Coffee Game so there is no need for you to calculate the interest or to keep very detailed records. Simply make sure that the recipient of foreign aid understands that interest *would be* accumulating on the full amount of each loan.

At the 1973 Conference of American States the Chairperson will again call on you to announce the sums of U.S. foreign aid that are available to the Latin American governments.

"In 1973 the United States will make the following sums of money available to the Representatives of Latin American governments in foreign aid:

— "To the *Government of Brazil* we offer *no foreign aid* this year because your coffee growers have foolishly gone through with their plans to process Brazilian coffee in Brazil;

— "To the *Government of Colombia* we again offer *75 cents* in foreign aid. The speed with which you are suppressing peasant rebellion indicates that our grants of military hardware are being well used. We again insist that you use 50 cents of the foreign aid loan for the purchase of more military hardware;

— "To the *Government of El Salvador* we offer *50 cents* in foreign aid under the same conditions as in 1972;

— "To the *Government of Guatemala* we offer *50 cents* in foreign aid. We wish that we could offer you more but popular reaction in the United States to our 'giveaway programs' of foreign aid have forced Congress to severely limit foreign aid spending this year;

— "To the *Government of Ecuador* we offer only *20 cents* in foreign aid this year. Though you have exhibited great restraint with regard to our fishing boats this past year we are unable to offer you the increased aid we promised you last year."

98

You are the CHAIRPERSON FOR
THE CONFERENCE OF AMERICAN STATES AND/OR
THE INTERNATIONAL COFFEE CONFERENCE

YOUR ROLE IN THE COFFEE GAME

The Director of the Coffee Game will ask you to chair the Conference of American States and /or the International Coffee Conference according to the following agendas.

AGENDA: Conference of American States

The Chairperson convenes the 1972 and 1973 Conferences of American States as soon as each government representative has had a chance to prepare the Year-End Financial Report for the respective year.

1. Call to order and introductions of the Government Representatives from each of the five Latin American countries: Brazil, Colombia, Ecuador, El Salvador, and Guatemala;

2. Word of welcome to any of the U.S. Agents or Representatives of the Latin American Coffee Growers' Organizations who may be in attendance at the Conference;

3. Call for the Year-End Statements to be read by each country; have an assistant record the information in the Statements on a chart visible to all:

    (a) How much money did you take in this year?
    (b) How much money did you have to pay out this year?
    (c) How much money do you owe the banks?
    (d) In a word or two how would you describe your general situation?

4. Ask the U.S. Export Agent to announce the dollar amounts of exports from the United States to each of the five Latin American countries and have the Agent explain any rise or fall in this price of U.S. exports;

5. Ask the U.S. Foreign Aid Official to advise each of the Latin American countries how much U.S. aid will be available to them in the coming year;

6. Instruct the countries to pay the U.S. Export Agent immediatetly *after* the International Coffee Conferences for that year (NOTE: the *ICC*, not the CAS!):

7. Explain to the Representatives of each of the countries that payment for their exports to the United States for the coming year will be available

from the U.S. Import Agent after—and only *after*—they have paid the U.S. Export Agent what they owe;

8. Announce that the International Coffee Conference will follow immediately upon the adjournment of the Conference of American States;

9. Adjourn the CAS for this year.

AGENDA: International Coffee Conference

The Chairperson convenes the 1972 and 1973 International Coffee Conferences immediately *after* the adjournment of the Conferences of American States in each of the years.

1. Call to order and introductions of the Representatives of the Coffee Growers' Organizations of each of the five Latin American countries: Brazil, Colombia, Ecuador, El Salvador, and Guatemala;

2. Word of welcome to any of the U.S. Agents or Representatives of the Latin American governments who may be in attendance at the Conference;

3. Call for the Year-End Statements to be read by each Representative; have an assistant record the information in the Statements on a chart visible to all:

   (a) How much money did you take in this year?
   (b) How much money did you have to pay out this year?
   (c) How much money do you owe the banks?
   (d) In a word or two how would you describe your general situation?

4. Instruct the U.S. Import Agent to quote the terms of the Coffee Agreement for the respective year (1972 or 1973);

5. Advise the Representatives of the Coffee Growers' Organizations that payment for their exports will be available from the U.S. Import Agent immediately after the ICC;

6. Adjourn the ICC for this year.

The Money Game

What would it be like to play the role
of a country for awhile? What political alliances
would we make? How would we allocate money?

Exercise

Follow the directions on the Player's Sheet.

PLAYER'S SHEET

The Money Game simulates an international meeting of industrialized and developing nations called to determine how $330 million should best be spent for development. Its purpose is to sharpen our understanding of international development and the realities of the rich/poor world in which we live. You will be asked to play one of these countries:

Algeria	Guatemala
Brazil	Indonesia
Canada	Jamaica
Ceylon	Tanzania
Cuba	United Kingdom
France	United States
Ghana	U.S.S.R.

Preparation:

Here are suggestions for getting a real feel for "your" country:

1. Begin with the library. Check indices for recent newspapers and periodicals. In the *Reader's Guide* find the listing for the country; also check topical listings such as "foreign trade," "gross national product (GNP)," etc. A nearby college or university may have additional resources in its library and among its student body and faculty (history, political science, international relations, economics or area studies). Consulates or trade missions in large cities have information available if you write or visit. You may also wish to write the embassy of "your" country in Washington, D.C.

2. Describe the country. What were the main events of its history which affect it today? Describe its geography and people. What are the main agricultural and manufactured products for national use and for export?

3. Know the developmental goal, governing philosophy and economic system of "your" country (e.g., U.S.: capitalism, Tanzania: socialism). Try to understand the beliefs of "your" country's "system." If you are representing (a) a rich country: How do your national goals affect "poor" countries? (b) a poor country: How does your nation actually help the populace achieve its development goal? What are the priorities for development? What are obstacles to progress?

4. Foreign Assistance: If you are representing (a) a rich country: What type of assistance (economic, social, cultural and/or military) do you give other nations in general? Those attending this meeting? What are the terms or conditions of your assistance? Do you get any "benefits" or returns from this assistance, e.g. prestige, political influence, expansion of your own markets, interest on loans or purchase of manufactured goods and equipment, etc.? How would you prefer that the conference fund be spent? (b) a

poor country: What type of assistance (economic, social, cultural, and/or military) do you get from any of the nations attending this conference? How difficult or easy was it to get? How has this assistance aided in the achievement of your development goals? How is assistance from different sources (e.g. church, U.N., foreign governments) similar? How is it different? How would you prefer that the conference fund be used?

5. Think how "your" country would use all or some of the $330 million fund.

6. Decide who your political and/or economic "allies" are among the nations represented. Why? Who are your political and/or economic "competitors" among these nations? Why?

7. Clip items from newspapers and magazines for the next few weeks that are relevant to "your" country; add these to your information folder. Look carefully through the financial sections.

8. Find some products in your local supermarket that come from the country you represent.

9. Become acquainted with the other countries attending the conference. Check in an encyclopedia or almanac; note current, pertinent news items.

10. Practice getting into your role by consciously reacting to news and events as if you were an Algerian, a Brazilian, a Canadian, etc.

Round I: How the Money Moves

PURPOSE.   To represent symbolically some annual economic interactions between rich and poor countries.

PLAYERS.   One conference chairperson, country delegations (of at least two people each), members of the press or other media. Delegates will elect a country to chair the meeting. A delegate from that country will then serve as chairperson and take a seat at the head table. Each delegate will contribute $1 (collected by the chairperson) to play the game to its finish. The chairperson will confer with the game director about the next steps in the game.

ACTION.   The chairperson will go through the economic life of the countries present in symbolic fashion. Money will pass between countries to illustrate how funds flow in the real markets of the world. The money remaining is the "Conference Fund." The work of the Conference is allocation of the fund. Discuss the transactions: Where did the money go? How did players feel about their role? About their country? About the other countries? Copies of the statistics chart used in this round, "How World Wealth is Divided," will be displayed to everyone when the round is *completely* over. Definitions of economic terms will be reviewed.

Round II: Getting to Know "My" Country

PURPOSE.   To put yourself "inside" the country you represent, to become increasingly familiar with "your" country's needs, priorities, internal and external problems, giving particular attention to trade and national development.

ACTION.   Each delegation will gather resources about its country. Study the findings again. There might be an opportunity for your delegation to interview someone knowledgeable from "your" country, or to ask questions of a conference resource person if one is available. Round II ends with a plenary session of the conference; each delegate will present a brief (3-5 minutes) statement about its national development objectives and needs. Delegates might discuss each country's expectations for the conference, possible general principles to govern allocation of the Conference Fund, etc. The adjournment of the plenary marks the end of this round. The chairperson announces the time of the next meeting.

News media reports may be made now (and periodically throughout the conference) either orally or as newsprint flash public announcements.

Round III: The Conference Debates

PURPOSE.   To draw up proposals for the use of the Conference Fund.

ACTION.   Decide first on a national objective/strategy for use of the Conference Fund. Review your opening statement, and discuss it in relation to those made by other delegations. What do you want most to do with the money? How can you get what you want? Which countries are with you? Which are against you? Where are you willing to compromise? Where are you determined to hold out no matter what?

After agreeing upon common strategy, members of each delegation should not stay together. Politic with other delegations; see what they are going to propose, with whom you might work, etc. Coalitions are essential. *At least two countries must sponsor each proposal for acceptance by the chairperson for consideration by the Conference.* Proposals must be presented in written form (printed on newsprint, or mimeographed, if possible). A delegate of one of the sponsoring nations will read each proposal to the Conference; each will be debated and voted upon in the order received. When the plenary begins, those submitting proposals should have an idea of antagonists and likely supporters when voting occurs.

In building coalitions, delegations should seek others with common needs and problems, perhaps even common enemies. Refer to statements made at the first plenary session to indicate where most countries stand on development issues.

Remember that there will be private motivating forces operating during these negotiations: anti-communist propaganda or bilateral ties of poorer countries with powerful, rich nations through loans and grants. Some possible proposal ideas are: ways to improve the terms of trade of one or more nations, commodity agreements on products of special economic value to a group of poor nations, schemes to use the Fund for regional, social, economic development, buffer funds, etc.

Round IV: Reflection

PURPOSE.   To reflect on the game as a learning experience.

ACTION.   Open discussion stimulated perhaps by the questions below: What were your feelings as a delegate? Would you have preferred to represent another country? If so, why? Did you feel proud of "your" country? Why or why not?

Did you have any difficulties identifying with "your" country? If so, was it a personal difficulty or a result of a previous image you had of that country? If you didn't experience any difficulties, to what do you attribute the ease with which you identified with "your" country? How influential were you within your delegation? How powerful was your country at the Conference? In negotiating sessions? What issues became clearer to you? What did you notice about the relationship among rich countries? Among poor countries? Between rich and poor countries? How were agreements reached to co-sponsor proposals? What were conflicting interests? Where was compromise made? What were common interests? Did you see any parallels with the way groups operated in the game and the way groups work in your community? In the nation? How do you feel about the game's conclusion?

The War Game

What are the causes of war?
Who and what are the enemies of peace?

Background Reading:

From *The Bishops' Call for Peace and the Development of Peoples* (General Conference Statement, United Methodist Church).

The Nature of Peace

Peace is not simply the absence of war, a nuclear stalemate or combination of uneasy cease-fires. It is that emerging dynamic reality envisioned by prophets where spears and swords give way to implements of peace (Isa. 2:1- 4); where historic antagonists dwell together in trust (Isa. 11:4 -11); and where righteousness and justice prevail. There will be no peace with justice until unselfish and informed love are structured into political processes and international arrangements.

The enemies of peace are many. War results from a complex of personal, social, economic and political forces. If war is to be overcome its root causes must be isolated and dealt with.

The Enemies of Peace

(1) *Blind self-interest is an enemy of peace.* The history of war is a history of unbridled greed, ambition, and self-centeredness. Nations have been willing to gain their own security and advantage at the expense of other weaker nations. Humankind, obsessed with "rightness" and power, has sought to impose its will on all its surroundings. Self-aggrandizement has too often prevailed over human rights and international justice. Vain self-assertion has been humanity's "nature" and in no small measure it has shaped our "destiny."

The self-interest that gives birth to war is both personal and social. Policymakers are individuals. Their decisions are moral decisions. Whether they live in a tribal culture, a representative democracy or a totalitarian police state, they are individually responsible. By their greed and cowardice, silence and truculence, arrogance and apathy, they contribute to the dismemberment of true community.

But self-interest is also institutionalized. Nation-states, economic systems, political and military forces, and the structures of our corporate life, serving their own interests, become self-seeking antagonists destroying the unity of humankind.

(2) *Economic exploitation is an enemy of peace.* No economic system is divinely inspired and every economic system should be judged by the ethical imperatives of the gospel of Jesus Christ. Personal fulfillment and international stability are impossible in a world where two out of three people go to bed hungry every night and where the chasm between "haves" and "have nots" grows wider day by day.

One cannot understand current events without taking into account the colonial policies of an earlier era. World powers carved up continents and divided the spoils. Third World nations and underdeveloped peoples are now reacting with bitterness and suspicion toward those forces that systematically exploited their personal and natural resources.

The Third World is understandably concerned about American domination of the world market, is wary of strings-attached aid programs and is determined to assert its independent selfhood. The "super-powers" are the new imperialists. With networks of economic and military interests intruding into almost every land, they frustrate authentic self-determination, manipulate power relationships and disturb the essential ingredients of international community.

(3) *Racism is an enemy of peace.* Whether its attitudes and institutions disturb domestic tranquility, contravene justice or erupt in bloody skirmishes, racism stands opposed to every humanizing process. Racist presuppositions are implicit in Western attitudes and policies toward Asia, Africa, the Middle East and Latin America, as well as toward black, brown, yellow and red persons in subcultures controlled by white majorities.

(4) *Population explosion is an enemy of peace.* Nations often justify expansionist policies on the basis of overcrowded homelands.

Human congestion, linked with poverty, hunger and filth, gives rise to frustration, despair and violence.

In affluent societies, an increasing population intensifies the ecological crisis as wealth multiplies industrial waste, pollutes air and water and jeopardizes the delicate balance of nature.

Both poverty and wealth, when complicated by overpopulation, aggravate hostilities and negate human values.

(5) *Nation worship is an enemy of peace.* Insulated, self-serving nationalism must yield to genuine international cooperation if humanity is to survive. The unilateral intervention of superpowers in the affairs of smaller nations (Hungary, Vietnam, Laos, Cambodia, Czechoslovakia, the Dominican Republic and Guatemala) must be ended. International anarchy is the most dangerous form of lawlessness confronting the human family today.

(6) *Continued reliance upon military violence is an enemy of peace.* There have been more war casualties in the twentieth century than in all previous centuries of recorded history combined. Nuclear and biochemical weaponry, and new, technological war-making equipment have thrust the human race into an indefensible posture. It is alleged that ninety percent of the war casualties in Indochina have been civilian. Old "just war" theories need to be carefully rethought in the light of present reality. Wars fought in the national interest will doubtless continue, but violence begets violence and in today's world extinction could result from irrational accident or momentary madness.

(7) *The arms race is an enemy of peace.* Arms races have always resulted in the utilization of their products. In spite of Strategic Arms Limitation Talks, the superpowers have continued with the development of ABM and anti-ABM hardware, and MIRV has been deployed. The current overkill capacities of the Soviet Union and the United States, coupled with the fact that there are now five nuclear powers, make future prospects for world harmony bleak indeed.

Dehumanization, a special threat in a materialistic, technocratic society, is implicit in almost all the "enemies of peace" we have outlined. The gospel of Jesus Christ proclaims the inestimable worth of each individual. It is "personal" in the most radical sense of the word. It seeks to humanize, and would make common cause with those values and forces that are working for the fulfillment of the human potential in today's world.

111

Haves and Have-Nots

What are the possibilities for community
when all power is concentrated in the hands of a few?

Background Reading:

From *Justice in the World* (Synod of Bishops)

The world in which the Church lives and acts is held captive by a tremendous paradox. Never before have the forces working for bringing about a unified world society appeared so powerful and dynamic; they are rooted in the awareness of the full basic equality as well as of the human dignity of all. Since men are members of the same human family, they are indissolubly linked with one another in the one destiny of the whole world, in the responsibility for which they all share.

The new technological possibilities are based upon the unity of science, on the global and simultaneous character of communications and on the birth of an absolutely interdependent economic world. Moreover, men are beginning to grasp a new and more radical dimension of unity; for they perceive that their resources, as well as the precious treasures of air and water—without which there cannot be life—and the delicate biosphere of the whole complex of all life on earth, are not infinite, but on the contrary must be saved and preserved as a unique patrimony belonging to all mankind.

The paradox lies in the fact that within this perspective of unity the forces of division and antagonism seem today to be increasing in strength. Ancient divisions between nations and empires, between races and classes, today possess new technological instruments of destruction. The arms race is a threat to man's highest good, which is life; it makes poor peoples and individuals yet more miserable, while making richer those already powerful; it creates a continuous danger of conflagration, and in the case of nuclear arms, it threatens to destroy all life from the face of the earth.

At the same time new divisions are being born to separate man from his neighbor. Unless combatted and overcome by social and political action, the influence of the new industrial and technological order favors the concentration of wealth, power and decision-making in the hands of a small public or private controlling group. Economic injustice and lack of social participation keep a man from attaining his basic human and civil rights.

In the last twenty-five years a hope has spread through the human race that economic growth would bring such a quantity of goods that it would be possible to feed the hungry at least with the crumbs falling from the table, but this has proved a vain hope in underdeveloped areas and in pockets of poverty in wealthier areas, because of the rapid growth of population and of the labor force, because of rural stagnation and the lack of agrarian reform, and because of the massive migratory flow to the cities, where the industries, even though endowed with huge sums of money, nevertheless provide so few jobs that not infrequently one worker in four is left unemployed. These stifling oppressions constantly give rise to great numbers of "marginal" persons, ill-fed, inhumanly housed, illiterate and deprived of political power as well as of the suitable means of acquiring responsibility and moral dignity.

Furthermore, such is the demand for resources and energy by the richer nations, whether capitalist or socialist, and such are the effects of dumping by them in the atmosphere and the sea that irreparable damage would be done to the essential elements of life on earth, such as air and water, if their high rates of consumption and pollution, which are constantly on the increase, were extended to the whole of mankind.

The strong drive towards global unity, the unequal distribution which places decisions concerning three quarters of income, investment and trade in the hands of one third of the human race, namely the more highly developed part, the insufficiency of a merely economic progress, and the new recognition of the material limits of the biosphere—all this makes us aware of the fact that in today's world new modes of understanding human dignity are arising.

Serfdom

What needs changing in society—
and how do we go about it?

Exercise

Read over "The Scenario" and the Roles and Goals in preparation for playing the simulation "Serfdom."

The Scenario

Once upon a time, there was a great king
who owned and ruled a vast land.
All the resources of the land,
property and people, belonged to him
and to whomever would succeed him as Ruler.
Because of his advancing age,
he decided to choose among his children
(princes and princesses)
which of them would be his successor.
So he set a task to test and prove each one of them.
In a space of five years
each was to build towers and fortresses
wherein the grain and treasures
of the country could be stored
and by which the land could be defended.
Each of the children was to decide
on a design for the buildings to be constructed
and would be rewarded
according to his or her accomplishments.
If one failed to measure up
to a minimal standard of accomplishment,
he/she would be executed, along with all assistants.
The child who succeeded most beyond the standards
would become the new Ruler
and all his/her assistants would become Lords.

Roles

There are 3 *Princes* who will choose 3 *Lords* to aid them in directing the work accomplishment. All others are *Serfs* who will do the actual work. A *Police Force* will see to it that law and order prevails throughout the simulation so that the tasks can be accomplished.

Goals

Participants are expected to acquire a given number of tokens (poker chips) by the end of the game in return for the work they do in fulfilling five specified tasks.

There will be five rounds; each round having its own rewards for task accomplishments. At the end of five rounds, each *Prince* must have acquired the minimum of 50 tokens; each *Lord* must have acquired 20 tokens; and each *Serf* must have acquired 10 tokens.

These goals remain with the individual as they are set at the start of the game. Even if a Lord is demoted by his Prince to a Serf he must still achieve the goal of 20 tokens by the end of the game. If at the end of the simulation, a Lord or a Serf has not reached the expected goals, then he is considered dead and all the tokens in his possession are forfeited to the Prince.

If at the end of the simulation a Prince has not achieved his standard, then he and all who worked with him are considered dead and all of their tokens are given to the new Ruler. The Prince who amasses the most tokens by the end of the game is declared the new Ruler.

Starpower and Powerplay

Who controls the power and wealth in society and for whose benefit is it used?

Background Reading:

From *World Justice and Peace: A Radical Analysis for American Christians* by L. McCulloch, T. Fenton, and E. Toland

Myth: Reforms of the capitalist system within the United States have brought about a more equitable distribution of wealth and power among our people than ever before.

Fact: The distribution of wealth in the United States is almost identical with the distribution of wealth in India. The only difference is that in the United States the economic pie is much bigger and so the results of this maldistribution are not quite as visible. Furthermore, with this wealth goes much of the control over the country's resources, industry, and public services.

In 1941, two-thirds of all manufacturing assets in the nation were controlled by 1,000 large corporations. Today a mere 200 giant corporations control this same percentage, i.e., a cool $350 billion. Despite the claim of "people's capitalism," these corporations are owned by less than 2% of the American population. According to the Lampman report, published in 1962, 80% of all corporate stocks was owned by the top 1.6% of the population, or 1.5 million people. Even more, the richest of the rich, the top 5% of this upper 1.6%, owned half of this group's stocks. Thus 75,000 people, each with assets of $500,000 or more, owned at least 40% of all corporate stock in the country!

Not only is the wealth of the nation, i.e., the factories, utilities, banks, etc., largely owned by a very small percentage of the population, but the yearly national income is equally maldistributed. According to a recent Brookings Institute study conducted by economist Joseph Pechman, the lowest fifth of American families receives only 3.2% of the national income while the highest fifth gets 45.8%, or more than fourteen times as much. Moreover, according to this study, the top 1% of American families receive more than twice the income of the 20% who occupy the bottom rung of the U.S. income ladder.

An even more revealing way to look at the economy is through the influence and control which a mere handful of multibillionaire families and financial groups have exerted for generations. The Rockefeller empire is not a thing of the past. Neither are the Dupont or Mellon trusts relics of another age. Again, precisely because these groups are anxious to keep the extent of their wealth from the public eye, accurate, up-to-date figures are not available. During the 1950's, however, several groups loomed on the economic horizon like elephants walking amidst ants. Although these groups regularly have interlocking interests in each other's area of influence, they are nevertheless distinguishable enough:

The *Morgan Guaranty Trust Group,* which included in its sphere of influence General Electric, International Nickel, Standard Brands, Campbell Soup, Coca Cola, Upjohns, Mutual Life Insurance Co. of N.Y., etc.

The *Rockefeller Group,* which included Chase Manhattan Bank, Equitable Life Insurance Co., Standard Oil of N.J., Eastern Airlines, General Foods, Borden, etc.

The *First National City Bank of N.Y. Group,* which included Boeing, United Aircraft, Anaconda Copper, National Cash Register, etc.

The *Mellon Group,* which included ALCOA, Gulf Oil, Westinghouse, etc.

The *Dupont Group,* which included Dupont Chemical, U.S. Rubber, Bendix Aviation, etc. (The Duponts recently had to sell their controlling interest in General Motors stock due to a court order. But the proceeds were merely reinvested in high growth, frequently defense-related industries.)

The *Chicago Group,* which unites many families, such as the McCormicks, the Deerings, the Nemours and the Fields, included the First National City Bank of Chicago, Continental Illinois National Bank, International Harvester, Sears Roebuck, Inland Steel, etc. Other families and groups, such as the Harrimans (Philadelphia), the Hannas (Cleveland), the Fords (Detroit), the Crockers (San Francisco), and the Hunts (Dallas) fill out the picture.

Although these families and groups compete with one another in trying to extend their spheres of influence, they also cooperate to run corporations that are too big for any one family or group to control. A good example is A.T.&T. On its board of directors are representatives of Chase Manhattan, First National City of N.Y., the Ford Foundation, the Chicago Group, and Morgan Guaranty Trust. It is truly a "collective possession" of the American upper class.

The effects of this concentration of wealth and power in the hands of a few are evident enough. A.T.&T., for example, is the largest private employer in the country, having over a million people on its payrolls. Forty-five percent of its employees however are paid less than $7,000 per year (before taxes). What is particularly interesting is that only 4% of Bell's white males earn so little whereas 64% of all Spanish-surnamed employees, 79% of all black employees, and 80% of all female employees earn less than $7,000 annually. Indeed, the Equal Employment Opportunity Commission had characterized A.T.&T. as "without doubt the largest oppressor of woman workers in the U.S."

And what is the response of A.T.&T.'s white male corporate elite to such obviously discriminatory practices? It is to fight desperately to maintain the present, very profitable, situation. The recent New York Telephone strike is a case in point. A.T.&T. used every means available to break the strike, principally by bringing in scab labor from New Jersey and other surrounding areas. As a result, after a several-months-long strike, the New York workers were forced to accept terms that were only $2 a week more than the company's pre-strike offer.

Does this mean A.T.&T. is short on cash? Hardly. In 1970 A.T.&T. paid out more than $3 billion to stock and bond holders. In comparison labor costs only amounted to about $7 billion—out of a total annual revenue of $18 billion paid for by phone users all over the country. When we examine who owns the largest shares of A.T.&T. stocks and bonds, we find once again that it is the upper 1.6% of the population. Maintaining this gravytrain, then, even at the cost of rising rates and poor service to customers and blatant exploitation of women and minority groups is in the best interest of A.T.&T.'s corporate elite.

119

Many similar examples could be given, in practically every industry from textiles to steel, from meat packing to gravedigging. Ultimately, however, the same simple fact emerges: money is power. Indeed, the power of the financial oligarchy in the United States rests specifically on the fact that it commands most of the country's money capital. The bank assets controlled by the main financial groups mentioned above are twice as large as the annual budget of the federal government. With this enormous wealth they dominate the American economy and determine its direction. Armed with the power to make key economic decisions concerning investments and the allocation of resources, they run their affairs and those of the nation according to the one rubric of corporate life: the maximization of profits.

Some Resources: Books, Action Guides, Education/Action Groups

Paperback Books

Development in a Divided World, edited by Dudley Seers and Leonard Joy (Baltimore: Penguin, 1971) $2.45. A very good selection of readings to introduce the topic of development.

The Great Ascent: The Struggle for Economic Development in Our Time by Robert L. Heilbroner (New York: Harper and Row, 1963) $1.60. A popular and readable introduction to issues of development such as aid and trade. Dated, but still worthwhile.

World Development: An Introductory Reader, edited by Hélène Castél (New York: Macmillan, 1971) $1.95. A varied collection of articles on the subject of world development.

The Enemy by Felix Greene (New York: Vintage, 1971) $1.95. An excellent introduction to the "why" of underdevelopment.

The Free World Colossus by David Horowitz (New York: Hill and Wang, 1971) $2.45. A history and critique of U.S. foreign policy in the Cold War.

The Radical Bible adapted from the German *bibel provokativ* by John Eagleson and Philip Scharper (Maryknoll, New York: Orbis Books, 1972) $1.95. The gospel's radical message of social justice juxtaposed with voices from the Third World describing their reality.

Property and Prophets: the Evolution of Economic Institutions and Ideologies by E.K. Hunt (New York: Harper and Row, 1972) $2.95. A very readable presentation of the development of capitalism—its defenders and opponents.

The Sick Society by Michael Tanzer (New York: Holt, Rinehart and Winston, 1971) $2.95. A radical "diagnosis" of U.S. society.

Child of the Dark: The Diary of Carolina Maria de Jesus (New York: New American Library, 1963) 95 cents. A moving personal diary of life in the slums of Sao Paulo, Brazil.

Fanshen: A Documentary of Revolution in a Chinese Village by William Hinton (New York: Vintage Books, 1966) $2.95. A personal report on the Chinese revolution from the viewpoint of the peasants in Long Bow Village in the late forties.

121

Guides for Action

Invest Yourself. The Commission on Voluntary Service and Action, 475 Riverside Drive, Room 665, New York, N.Y. 10027. A catalog of service opportunities published annually listing several hundred specific projects and placements with 26,000 openings, as well as the names and addresses of the 150 private, North American voluntary service agencies who individually sponsor service projects and who together make up CVSA. Price: $1 postpaid.

Target: Development Action. American Freedom from Hunger Foundation, 1717 H Street, N.W., Washington, D.C. 20006. A 90-page booklet filled with education and action ideas for youth. Price: $1.50.

Vocations for Social Change. VSC, Canyon, California 94516. VSC publishes a free bi-monthly 60-page listing of action projects and job opportunities for those concerned with social change and social justice particularly in the United States.

Youth Power Strategy Manual. Walther League, 875 N. Dearborn St., Chicago, Illinois 60610. The aim of this 28-page booklet is to help young people get used to experimenting and putting ideas into action within their local communities. Price: 50 cents.

Education/Action Groups

American Freedom from Hunger Foundation/Young World Development, 1717 H Street, N.W., Washington, D.C. 20006. AFFHF sponsors the annual "Walks for Development" and carries on various educational activities. YWD is their youth division.

American Friends Service Committee, 160 N. 15th Street, Philadelphia, Pa. 19102. The regional offices of AFSC are involved in four major areas: peace education, community relations, international affairs, and international service.

New World Coalition, 419 Boylston St., Room 209, Boston, Ma. 02116. NWC is developing programs to combine critical thinking and action on issues of social justice. Particular programs are a self-tax union, social marketing, and an education network.

OXFAM-America, 474 Centre St., Newton, Ma. 02158. The U.S. affiliate of OXFAM carries a sizeable selection of educational materials on issues of development.